SPURGEON'S SERMON ILLUSTRATIONS

T0204698

Other Kregel Titles by C. H. Spurgeon

Commenting and Commentaries
Spurgeon's Sermon Notes
The Treasury of David

SPURGEON'S SERMON ILLUSTRATIONS

CHARLES H. SPURGEON

KREGEL PUBLICATIONS
Grand Rapids, Michigan 49501

Spurgeon's Sermon Illustrations, by Charles H. Spurgeon, compiled and edited by David Otis Fuller. Published in 1990 by Kregel Publications, a division of Kregel, Inc., P.O. Box 2607, Grand Rapids, MI 49501. All rights reserved.

Cover Design: Don Ellens

Library of Congress Cataloging-in-Publication Data

Spurgeon, Charles H. (Charles Haddon), 1834–1892.
  [Sermon ilustrations]
  Spurgeon's sermon illustrations / compiled and edited by David Otis Fuller.
       p.   cm.
  Reprint. Originally published: C. H. Spurgeon's sermon illustrations. Grand Rapids, MI: Zondervan, 1942.

  1. Homiletical illustrations. 2. Baptists—Sermons.
I. Fuller, David Otis, 1903-1988. II. Title.

BV4225.S66 1990   251'.08—dc20   90-36549
                                          CIP

ISBN   0-8254-3767-9 (pbk.)

    1 2 3 4 5 Printing/Year 94 93 92 91 90

Printed in the United States of America

CONTENTS

SPURGEON'S SERMON ILLUSTRATIONS

SHORT SAYINGS OF C. H. SPURGEON

PREFACE

One of Spurgeon's old students, Dr. J. C. Carlile, once uttered this fitting eulogy of "the last of the Puritans": "England's greatest contribution to the spread of the Gospel in the nineteenth century was Charles Haddon Spurgeon. Through him God wrought signs and wonders, adding another chapter to the Acts of the Apostles. There is no class or type in which Spurgeon can be included. He stands alone, a new species among the varieties of ministers, a sun that outshines the stars in splendor."

These words are no exaggeration. We have felt this small endeavor a sacred privilege that has brought blessing and inspiration again and again. The very choicest illustrations and most striking phases have been taken from three volumes now long since out of print. There are over 550 illustrations and direct quotations in this volume, used during the mighty ministry of this intellectual and spiritual giant of God.

The life of Paul the apostle is striking in many ways. One of them is the way it begins and ends. Acts 9:20 tells us how he began—uplifting and magnifying Christ, "And straightway he preached Christ in the synagogues, that He is the Son of God." With that constancy and consistency, so rarely found in Christians, "the apostle to the Gentiles" finished his course in exactly the same way he began, Acts 28:30, 31, "And Paul dwelt two whole years in his own hired house, and received all that came in unto him, preaching the kingdom of God, and teaching those things which concern the Lord Jesus Christ, with all confidence, no man forbidding him."

The apostle to the London metropolis and the world in the last century, came no whit behind Paul in this respect.

Listen to a phrase from the first sermon he ever delivered in London, in the New Park Street Chapel, December 18th, 1853, at the age of nineteen, "Nor does God love me less now than when He gave that grand proof of love, His Son, Jesus Christ, to die for me. Even now He loves me with the same intensity as when He poured out the vials of justice on His darling to save rebel worms."

Nearly forty years later, June 7th, 1891, Mr. Spurgeon spoke for the last time from the platform of the Metropolitan tabernacle. And the last words he uttered in the pulpit were these:

"IF YOU WEAR THE LIVERY OF CHRIST, YOU WILL FIND HIM SO MEEK AND LOWLY OF HEART, THAT YOU WILL FIND REST UNTO YOUR SOULS. HE IS THE MOST MAGNANIMOUS OF CAPTAINS. THERE NEVER WAS HIS LIKE AMONG THE CHOICEST OF PRINCES. HE IS ALWAYS TO BE FOUND IN THE THICKEST PART OF THE BATTLE. WHEN THE WIND BLOWS COLD HE ALWAYS TAKES THE BLEAK SIDE OF THE HILL. THE HEAVIEST END OF THE CROSS LIES EVER ON HIS SHOULDERS. IF HE BIDS US CARRY A BURDEN, HE CARRIES IT ALSO. IF THERE IS ANYTHING THAT IS GRACIOUS, GENEROUS, KIND AND TENDER, YEA LAVISH AND SUPERABUNDANT IN LOVE, YOU ALWAYS FIND IT IN HIM. HIS SERVICE IS LIFE, PEACE, JOY. OH, THAT YOU WOULD ENTER ON IT AT ONCE! GOD HELP YOU TO ENLIST UNDER THE BANNER OF JESUS CHRIST!"

Reader, are you saved for Eternity? If so, may God help you and me to be as faithful as Charles Haddon Spurgeon to our Sovereign God and Saviour, Jesus Christ.

DAVID OTIS FULLER.

SPURGEON'S SERMON ILLUSTRATIONS

AFFLICTION—BLESSED

The bow of trouble shot David like an arrow toward God! It is a blessed thing when the waves of affliction wash us upon the rock of confidence in God alone, when darkness below gives us an eye to the light above.

* * * * * *

AFFLICTION—ATTENDANT UPON HONOR

In the ancient times, a box on the ear given by a master to a slave meant liberty, little would the freedman care how hard was the blow. By a stroke from the sword the warrior was knighted by his monarch, small matter was it to the new-made knight if the royal hand was heavy.

When the Lord intends to lift His servants into a higher stage of spiritual life, He frequently sends them a severe trial; He makes His Jacobs to be prevailing princes, but He confers the honor after a night of wrestling, and accompanies it with a shrunken sinew. Be it so, who among us would wish to be deprived of the trials if they are the necessary attendants of spiritual advancement?

* * * * * *

AFFLICTION—AWAKENING GRATITUDE

Afflictions when sanctified make us grateful for mercies which aforetime we treated with indifference. We sat for half an hour in a calf's shed the other day, quite grateful for the shelter from the driving rain, yet at no other time would we have entered such a hovel.

Discontented persons need a course of the bread of adversity and the water of affliction, to cure them of the

wretched habit of murmuring. Even things which we
loathed before, we shall learn to prize when in troublous
circumstances. We are no lovers of lizards, and yet at
Pont St. Martin, in the Val D'Aosta, where the mosquitoes,
flies and insects of all sorts drove us nearly to distraction,
we prized the little green fellows, and felt quite an attach-
ment to them as they darted out their tongues and devoured
our worrying enemies.

Sweet are the uses of adversity, and this among them—
that it brings into proper estimation mercies aforetime
lightly esteemed.

* * * * * *

AFFLICTION—An Incentive to Zeal

There is an old story in the Greek annals of a soldier
under Antigonus who had a disease about him, an extremely
painful one, likely to bring him soon to the grave. Always
first in the charge was this soldier, rushing into the hottest
part of the fray, as the bravest of the brave. His pain
prompted him to fight, that he might forget it; and he
feared not death, because he knew that in any case he had
not long to live. Antigonus, who greatly admired the
valour of his soldier, discovering his malady, had him cured
by one of the most eminent physicians of the day; but, alas!
from that moment the warrior was absent from the front
of the battle. He now sought his ease; for, as he remarked
to his companions, he had something worth living for—
health, home, family, and other comforts, and he would not
risk his life now as aforetime.

So, when our troubles are many we are often by grace
made courageous in serving our God; we feel that we have
nothing to live for in this world, and we are driven, by
hope of the world to come, to exhibit zeal, self-denial and
industry. But how often is it otherwise in better times!

for then the joys and pleasures of this world make it hard for us to remember the world to come, and we sink into inglorious ease.

* * * * * *

AGE—No Cure for Sin

According to Aesop, an old woman found an empty jar which had lately been full of prime old wine, and which still retained the fragrant smell of its former contents. She greedily placed it several times to her nose, and drawing it backwards and forwards said, "Oh, most delicious! How nice must the wine itself have been, when it leaves behind in the very vessel which contained it so sweet a perfume!"

Men often hug their vices when their power to enjoy them is gone. The memories of revelling and wantonness appear to be sweet to the ungodly in their old age. They sniff the empty bottles of their follies, and only wish they could again be drunken with them. Age cures not the evil heart, but exhibits in a ridiculous but deeply painful light the indelible perversity of human nature.

* * * * * *

ANGELS—Ministering

I have often admired the language of Mohammed, when in the battle of Ohod he said to his followers, pointing to their foes, "Charge them! I can hear the wings of angels as they hasten to our help." That was a delusion on his part, for he and his men were badly beaten; but it is no delusion in the case of the servants of Christ. We can hear the wings of angels. Providence is always working with you while you are working for God.

* * * * * *

ANGER—Inventive

Man can always find ways of sinning against God. I remember, in my younger days, a school-boy who, when at play with his companions, would fly into furious passions, and would at once throw something at the person with whom he was angry; and the point I noticed was that he always had something to throw. Let him be in the school-room, playground, or in the street, there would surely be a stone, or a book, or a slate, or a cup ready to his hand.

So it is with men who fight against the Lord; they discover weapons everywhere, in the fury of their rebellion. The evil brain is quick in devising, the depraved ear is swift in apprehending, and the sinful hand is deft in carrying out any and every scheme of disobedience to the Lord.

* * * * * *

BAPTISM

The tendency everywhere is to say, "Baptism should not be mentioned; it is sectarian." Who said so? If our Lord commanded it who dares to call it sectarian? We are not commanded to preach a part of the Gospel, but the whole of the Gospel.

* * * * * *

BAPTISM—Spurgeon's

To me, it is a solemn memory that I professed my faith openly in baptism. Vividly do I recall the scene. It was the third of May, and the weather was cold because of a keen wind. I see the broad river, and the crowds which lined the banks, and the company upon the ferry-boat. The Word of the Lord was preached by a man of God who is now gone home; and when he had so done, he went down into the water, and we followed him, and he baptized us. I remember how, after being the slave of timidity, I rose from the liquid grave quickened into holy courage by that one act of decision, consecrated henceforth to bear a life-long testimony. By an avowed death to the world I professed my desire henceforth to live with Jesus, for Jesus, and like Jesus.

* * * * * *

BELIEVING OUR LIVING

You cannot live without faith: for again and again we are told—"The just shall live by faith." Believing is our living, and we, therefore, need it always. And if God give thee great faith, my dear brother, thou must expect great trials; for, in proportion as thy faith shall grow, thou wilt have to do more, and endure more. Little boats may keep close to shore, as becomes little boats; but if God make thee a great vessel, and load thee with a rich freight, He means that thou shouldst know what great billows are, and should feel their fury till thou seest "His wonders in the deep."

* * * * * *

BELIEVERS LOYALTY

Have you never heard of the dying and wounded in Napoleon's wars who still clung to their Emperor with an idolatrous love in the hour of death? Lifting himself upon his elbow, the soldier of the Old Guard gave one more cheer for the great captain. If the dying warrior saw Napoleon riding over the field, he would with his last gasp, cry, "Vive l'Empereur!" and then expire. We read of one, that when the surgeons were trying to extract a bullet from his chest, he said, "Go a little deeper and you will find the Emperor." He had him on his heart. Infinitely more commendable is the loyalty of the believer to the Lord Christ.

* * * * * *

BIBLE—Quote Accurately

I heard a brother in a prayer-meeting say, "The Lord hath done great things for us, whereof we *desire to be* glad";

and I wanted to jump down that man's throat and pull that passage back again and put it into its natural shape.

* * * * * *

BIBLE—Neglected

The last new book, perhaps the last sentimental story, will win attentive reading, when the divine, mysterious, unutterable depths of heavenly knowledge are disregarded by us. Alas, my brethren, too many eat the unripe fruit of the vineyards of Satan, and the fruits of the Lord's vines they utterly despise!

* * * * * *

THE BIBLE—God's Word

There is an essential difference between man's word and God's word, and it is fatal to mistake the one for the other. If you receive even the Gospel as the word of men you cannot get the blessing out of it, for the sweetness of the Gospel lies in the confidence of our heart that this is the Word of God.

* * * * * *

BIBLE—Cause of Interest in It

The lifeboat may have a tasteful bend and beautiful decoration, but these are not the qualities for which I prize it; it was my salvation from the howling sea! So the interest which a regenerate soul takes in the Bible, is founded on a personal application to the heart of the saving truth which it contains. If there is no taste for this truth, there can be no relish for the Scriptures.—*F. W. Alexander, D.D.*

* * * * * *

BIBLE—Why Priests Withhold It

The true reason why the Papists forbid the Scriptures to be read is not to keep men from errors and heresies, but to keep them from discovering those which they themselves impose upon them. Such trash as they trade in would never go off their hands if they did not keep their shops thus dark; which made one of their shavelings so bitterly complain of Luther for spoiling their market, saying that but for him they might have persuaded the people of Germany to eat hay. Anything, indeed, will go down a blind man's throat.—*Gurnal*.

* * * * * *

CHASTISEMENT—Proof of Love

Mr. Rutherford, writing to a lady who had lost five children and her husband, says to her, "Oh, how Christ must love you! He would take every bit of your heart to Himself. He would not permit you to reserve any of your soul for any earthly thing." Can we stand that test? Can we let all go for His sake?

* * * * * *

CHILDREN—Their Future

In the early French revolution, the schoolboys of Bourges, from twelve to seventeen years of age, formed themselves into a Band of Hope. They wore a uniform, and were taught drill. On their holidays, their flag was unfurled, displaying in shining letters the sentence — "TREMBLEZ, TYRANS, NOUS GRANDIRONS!" (Tremble, Tyrants, we shall grow up!) Without any charge of spurious enthusiasm, we may, in imagination, hear the shouts of confidence and courage, uttered by the young Christians of the future, as they say, "Tremble, O enemy, we are growing up for God!"— *Mr. S. R. Pattison's Address at the Meeting of the Baptist Union, 1869.*

* * * * * *

CHRIST FOR ALL

I recollect in Martin Luther's life that he saw, in one of
the Romish Churches, a picture of the Pope, and the
Cardinals, and bishops, and priests, and monks, and friars,
all on board a ship. They were all safe, every one of them.
As for the laity, poor wretches, they were struggling in the
sea, and many of them drowning. Only those were saved
to whom the good men in the ship were so kind as to hand
out a rope or a plank.

That is not our Lord's teaching: His blood is shed "for
many," and not for the few. He is not the Christ of a
caste, or a class, but the Christ of all conditions of men.
His blood is shed for many sinners, that their sins may be
remitted.

* * * * * *

CHRIST THE WAY

A minister in America some time ago was going up the
aisle of his church during a revival, when a young man
earnestly cried to him, "Sir, can you tell me the way to
Christ?" "No," was the answer, very deliberately given;
"I cannot tell you the way to Christ." The young man
answered, "I beg pardon; I thought you were a minister of
the gospel." "So I am," was the reply. "How is it that
you cannot tell me the way to Christ?" "My friend," said
the minister, "there is no way to Christ. He is Himself the
way. All who believe in Him are justified from all things.
There is no way to Christ; Christ is here."

* * * * * *

CHRIST—Refuses None

I have preached His Gospel now for many years, but I
never met with a sinner yet that Christ refused to cleanse
when he came to Him. I never knew of a single case of a

man who trusted Jesus, and asked to be forgiven, confessing his sin and forsaking it, who was cast out. I say I never met with one man whom Jesus refused; nor shall I ever do so. I have spoken with harlots whom He has restored to purity, and drunkards whom He has delivered from their evil habit, and with men guilty of foul sins who have become pure and chaste through the grace of our Lord Jesus. They have always told me the same story—"I sought the Lord, and He heard me; He hath washed me in His blood and I am whiter than snow."

* * * * * *

CHRIST—The Soul's Only Defence

There is an ancient parable which says that the dove once made a piteous complaint to her fellow birds, that the hawk was a most cruel tyrant, and was thirsting for her blood. One counselled her to keep below—but the hawk can stoop for its prey; another advised her to soar aloft—but the hawk can mount as high as she. A third bade her hide herself in the woods, but alas! these are the hawk's own estates, where he holds his court. A fourth recommended her to keep in the town, but there man hunted her, and she feared that her eyes would be put out by the cruel falconer to make sport for the hawk. At last one told her to rest herself in the clefts of the rock, there she would be safe, violence itself could not surprise her there.

The meaning is easy; reader, do not fail to catch it, and to act upon it. The dove is thy poor defenceless soul. Satan is thy cruel foe; wouldst thou not escape from him? Thy poverty can not protect thee, for sin can stoop to the poor man's level and devour him in the cottage, and drag him to hell from a hovel. Thy riches are no security, for Satan can make these a snare to thee, and if thou shouldst mount ever so high, the bird of prey can follow thee and rend thee in pieces! The busy world with all its cares cannot shelter thee, for here it is that the great enemy is most at home; he is the prince of this world, and seizes men who find their joys as easily as a kite lays hold upon a sparrow. Nor can retirement secure you, for there are sins peculiar to quietude, and hell's dread vulture soars over lonely solitudes to find defenceless souls, and rend them in pieces. There is but one defence. O may you and I fly to it at once! Jesus was wounded for sin; faith in Him saves at once and for ever.

* * * * * *

CHRISTIANS—All One

Well may we be called brethren, for we are redeemed by one Blood; we are partakers of the same life; we feed upon the same heavenly food; we are united to the same living Head; we seek the same ends; we love the same Father; we are heirs of the same promises, and we shall dwell forever together in the same heaven.

* * * * * *

CHRISTIANS—Neglectful of Means of Grace

At a prayer-meeting, some time ago, one brother prayed that the Lord would bless those who were at home on beds of sickness and on sofas of wellness. The last words were unexpected, but very needful.

* * * * * *

CHRIST—Lost

Did you lose Christ by sin? You will find Christ in no other way but by the giving up of the sin and seeking by the Holy Spirit to mortify the member in which the lust doth dwell. Did you lose Christ by neglecting the Scriptures? You must find Christ in the Scriptures. It is a true proverb, "Look for a thing where you dropped it; it is there." So look for Christ where you lost Him, for He has not gone away.

* * * * * *

CHRIST—The Preacher's Theme

The pulpit is intended to be a pedestal for the cross, though, alas! even the cross itself, it is to be feared, is sometimes used as a mere pedestal for the preacher's fame. We may roll the thunders of eloquence, we may dart the coruscations of genius, we may scatter the flowers of poetry, we may diffuse the light of science, we may enforce the precepts of morality, from the pulpit; but if we do not make Christ the great subject of our preaching, we have forgotten our errand, and shall do no good. Satan trembles at nothing but the cross: at this he does tremble; and if we would destroy his power, and extend that holy and benevolent kingdom, which is righteousness, peace and joy in the Holy Ghost, it must be by means of the cross.—*F. A. Fames.*

* * * * * *

CHRIST JESUS—The Marrow of Theology

The late venerable and godly Dr. Archibald Alexander, of Princeton, United States, had been a preacher of Christ for sixty years, and a professor of divinity for forty. He died on the 22nd of October, 1851. On his death-bed, he was heard to say to a friend, "All my theology is reduced to this narrow compass—Jesus Christ came into the world to save sinners."

* * * * * *

GLOOMY CHRISTIANS

I am bound to mention among the curiosities of the churches, that I have known many deeply spiritual Christian people who have been afraid to rejoice. Much genuine religion has been "sicklied o'er with the pale cast of thought!" Some take such a view of religion that it is to them a sacred duty to be gloomy.

* * * * * *

CHRISTIANS

Does it not mean that we are in Christ as the birds are in the air, which buoys them up and enables them to fly? Are we not in Christ as the fish are in the sea? Our Lord has become our element, vital, and all surrounding. In Him we live, and move, and have our being. He is in us and we are in Him. Without Him we can do nothing and we are nothing. Thus are we emphatically in Him.

* * * * * *

CHRISTIANS—Some Like Old China

My venerated grandmother owned a set of choice china, a part of which, I believe, is in use now. Why does it exist now? It has seen little service. It only came out on high days and holidays, say once in six months, when ministers and friends came to tea. It was a very nice set of old china, too good for children to break.

Some Christians are like that fine old ware, it would not do to use them too often. They are too good for every day. They do not teach their servants, and try to win the poor people in their neighborhood to Christ. But they talk well at a conference.

Oh! you fine bits of eggshell china, I know you. Don't fear. I am not going to break you; yet I would somewhat trouble you by the remark, that in the case of such ware as you are, more pieces get broken in the cupboard than on the table. You will last longer if you get to work for Christ in every-day work. Jesus was not sent out for particular occasions, neither are you.

* * * * * *

CHURCH—Love for Christ

The Church is the bride of Christ, and for a bride to fail in love is to fail in all things. It is idle for the wife to say that she is obedient, and so forth; if love to her husband has evaporated, her wifely duty cannot be fulfilled; she has lost the very life and soul of the marriage state. So, my brethren, this is a most important matter, our love to Christ, because it touches the very heart of that communion with Him which is the crown and essence of our spiritual life. As a church, we must love Jesus or else we have lost our reason for existence. Lose love, lose all. Leave our first love, we have left strength and peace and joy and holiness.

* * * * * *

CHURCH—A Dead

A dead church is a reeking Golgotha, a breeding place of evils, a home of devils. The tombs may be newly white-washed, but they are none the less open sepulchres, haunts of unclean spirits.

A church all alive is a little heaven, the resort of angels, the temple of the Holy Ghost. In some of our churches everybody seems to be a little colder than anybody else. The members are holy icicles. A general frost has paralyzed everybody; and though some are colder than others, yet all are below zero.

* * * * * *

COMING TO CHRIST—As a Sinner

A great monarch was accustomed on certain set occasions to entertain all the beggars of the city. Around him were placed his courtiers, all clothed in rich apparel; the beggars sat at the same table in their rags of poverty. Now it came to pass, that on a certain day, one of the courtiers had spoiled his silken apparel, so that he dared not put it on, and he felt, "I cannot go to the king's feast today, for my robe is foul." He sat weeping till the thought struck him, "Tomorrow when the king holds his feast, some will come as courtiers happily decked in their beautiful array, but others will come and be made quite as welcome who will be dressed in rags. "Well, well," said he, "so long as I may see the king's face, and sit at the royal table, I will enter among the beggars." So without mourning because he had lost his silken habit, he put on the rags of a beggar, and he saw the king's face as well as if he had worn his scarlet and fine linen.

My soul has done this full many a time, when her evidences of salvation have been dim; and I bid you do the same when you are in like case: if you cannot come to Jesus as a saint, come as a sinner; only do come with simple faith to Him, and you shall receive joy and peace.

* * * * * *

COMMUNION OF SAINTS

What the circulation of the blood is to the human body, that the Holy Spirit is to the body of Christ which is the church. Now, by virtue of the one life-blood, every limb of the body holds fellowship with every other, and as long as life lasts that fellowship is inevitable. If the hand be unwashed the eye cannot refuse communion with it on that account; if the finger be diseased the hand cannot, by binding a cord around it, prevent the life-current from flowing. Nothing but death can break up the fellowship; you must tear away the member, or it must of necessity commune with the rest of the body.

It is even thus in the body of Christ; no laws can prevent one living member of Christ from fellowship with every other, the pulse of living fellowship sends a wave through the whole mystical frame; where there is but one life, fellowship is an inevitable consequence. Yet some talk of restricted communion, and imagine that they can practice it.

* * * * * *

CONVERSIONS (Sudden)—NOT ALL GENUINE

Fish sometimes leap out of the water with great energy, but it would be foolish to conclude that they have left the liquid element for ever. In a moment they are swimming again as if they had never forsaken the stream; indeed, it was but a fly that tempted them aloft, or a sudden freak; the water is still their home, sweet home.

When we see long-accustomed sinners making a sudden leap at religion, we may not make too sure that they are converts; perhaps some gain allures them, or sudden excitement stirs them, and if so they will be back again at their old sins. Let us hope well, but let us not commend too soon.

* * * * * *

CONVERSION—REMARKABLE

There was one who went to hear Mr. Whitefield—a member of the "Hell-fire Club," a desperate fellow. He stood up at the next meeting of his abominable associates, and he delivered Mr. Whitefield's sermon with wonderful accuracy, imitating his very tone and manner. In the middle of his exhortation he converted himself, and came to a sudden pause, sat down broken-hearted, and confessed the power of the gospel. That club was dissolved.

That remarkable convert was Mr. Thorpe, of Bristol, whom God so greatly used afterwards in the salvation of others. I would rather have you read the Bible to mock at it than not read it at all. I would rather that you came to hear the Word of God out of hatred to it than you never came at all.

* * * * * *

CORRUPTIONS—HARD TO DIE

A cat once sprang at my lips while I was talking, and bit me savagely. My friend in whose house it occurred decreed that the poor creature should die. The sentence he executed personally, to the best of his ability, and threw the carcass away. To his surprise, the cat walked into the house the next day.

Often and often have I vowed death to some evil propensity, and have fondly dreamed that the sentence was fulfilled, but alas! in weaker moments I have had sad cause to know that the sinful tendency still survived.

* * * * * *

CORRUPTIONS—SEEN EVEN IN SOLITUDE

George Shadford wrote: "One day a friend took me to see a hermit in the woods. After some difficulty we found his hermitage, which was a little place like a hog-sty, built of several pieces of wood, covered with bark of trees, and his bed consisted of dry leaves. There was a narrow beaten path about twenty or thirty yards in length by the side of it, where he frequently walked to meditate."

"If one offered him food, he would take it, but if money was offered him, he would be angry. If anything was spoken which he did not like, he broke out into a violent passion. He had lived in this cell seven cold winters, and after all his prayers, counting his beads, and separating from the rest of mankind, still corrupt nature was all alive within him."

Alas! alas! what will it avail us whether we are in England or Ireland, Scotland or America; whether we live amongst mankind, or retire into a hermitage, if we still carry with us our own hell, our corrupt evil tempers? Without a new heart and a right spirit, no condition can deliver a man from the thraldom of his sins. Neither publicity nor solitude avails anything until grace prevails with us. The devil can tempt in the wilderness as well as in the crowd. We want not hermitages but heavenly-mindedness.

* * * * * *

CONSOLATION

When two Christians met together who were sitting under a very lean and starving ministry, one of them comforted his fellow concerning the miserable discourse by saying: "Never mind, my friend, there is not much in the sermon, but the text is a feast by itself."

* * * * * *

CUTTLE-FISH—Persons Who Resemble a

It was an old Pythagorean maxim, "Sepiam ne edito," "never eat a cuttle-fish." The cuttle-fish has the power of emitting a black liquid which dyes the water and enables it to conceal itself. Have nothing to do with those who darken all around them that they themselves may be unseen; honest men love light, and only the evil find darkness to be congenial. When an author is too obscure to be understood, leave him till he knows how to write; when a preacher is mystical, high-flown, sophistical, shun him, for it is most likely he labours to conceal some latent heresy; when a man's policy is deep and artful, flee from him, for he means no good. No deceiver or double-tongued man must be admitted within the circle of your confidence. Remember the advice, never eat a cuttle-fish.

* * * * * *

DEATH

There are ten thousand gates to death. One man is choked by a grape-stone, another dies through sleeping in a newly whitewashed room; one receives death as he passes by a reeking sewer, another finds it in the best kept house or by a chill taken in a walk. Those who study neither to eat nor to drink anything unwholesome, nor go into quarters where the arrows of death are flying, yet pass away on a sudden, falling from their couch into a coffin, from their seat into the sepulchre.

* * * * * *

DEATH

The hour of death may be fitly likened to that celebrated picture in the National Gallery, of Perseus holding up the head of Medusa. That head turned all persons into stone who looked upon it. There is a warrior represented with a dart in his hand; he stands stiffened, turned into stone, with the javelin even in his fist. There is another with a poignard beneath his robe, about to stab; he is now the statue of an assassin, motionless and cold. Another is creeping along stealthily, like a man in ambuscade, and there he stands a consolidated rock; he has looked only upon that head, and he is frozen into stone.

Such is death. What I am when death is held before me, that I must be forever. When my spirit departs, if God finds me hymning His praise, I shall hymn it in heaven; if He finds me breathing out oaths, I shall follow up those oaths in hell.

* * * * * *

DECISION FOR CHRIST

After the disgraceful defeat of the Romans, at the battle of Allia, Rome was sacked, and it seemed as if, at any moment, the Gauls might take the Capitol. Among the garrison was a young man of the Fabian family, and on a certain day the anniversary of a sacrifice returned, when his family had always offered sacrifice upon the Quirinal

Hill. This hill was in the possession of the Gauls; but when the morning dawned, the young man took the sacred utensils of his god, went down from the Capitol, passed through the Gallic sentries, through the main body, up the hill, offered sacrifice, and came back unharmed. It was always told as a wonder among Roman legends.

This is just how the Christian should act when decision for Christ is called for. Though he be a solitary man in the midst of a thousand opponents, let him, at the precise moment when duty calls, fearless of all danger, go straight to the appointed spot, do his duty, and remember that consequences belong to God, and not to us. I pray God that after this style we may witness for Christ.

* * * * * *

DECISION—Needed

If confessors, reformers, martyrs and covenanters had been recreant to the name and faith of Jesus, where would have been the churches of today? Must we not play the man as they did? If we do not, are we not censuring our fathers?

It is very pretty, is it not, to read of Luther and his brave deeds? Of course, everybody admires Luther! Yes, yes; but you do not want anyone else to do the same today. When you go to the Zoological Gardens you all admire the bear; but how would you like a bear at home, or a bear wandering loose about the streets? You tell me that it would be unbearable, and no doubt you are right.

So, we admire a man who was firm in the faith, say four hundred years ago; the past ages are a sort of bear-pit or iron cage for him; but such a man today is a nuisance, and must be put down. Call him a narrow-minded bigot, or give him a worse name if you can think of one. Yet imagine that in those ages past, Luther, Zwingle, Calvin, and their compeers had said, "The world is out of order; but if we try to set it right we shall only make a great row, and get ourselves into disgrace. Let us go to our chambers, put on our nightcaps, and sleep over the bad times, and perhaps when we wake up things will have grown better." Such conduct on their part would have entailed upon us a heritage of error. Age after age would have gone down into the infernal deeps, and the pestiferous bogs of error would have swallowed all. These men loved the faith and the name of Jesus too well to see them trampled on. Note what we owe them, and let us pay to our sons the debt we owe to our fathers.

It is today as it was in the Reformers' days. Decision is needed. Here is the day for the man, where is the man for the day? We who have had the gospel passed to us by martyr hands dare not trifle with it, nor sit by and hear it denied by traitors, who pretend to love it, but inwardly abhor every line of it. The faith I hold bears upon it marks of the blood of my ancestors.

* * * * * *

DESPONDENCY

Colton declares that in moments of despondency Shakespeare thought himself no poet; and Raphael doubted his right to be called a painter. We call such self-suspicions morbid, and ascribe them to a hypochondriacal fit; in what other way can we speak of those doubts as to their saintship, which occasionally afflict the most eminently holy of the Lord's people!

* * * * * *

DEVOTION—WHOLE-HEARTED

The pearl fisher standing on the rocks plunges deep into the sea; he does not know whether or no he shall bring up a pearl that will decorate an emperor's diadem, but he searches the deeps in that hope: and why should not he bring up such a treasure as well as anybody else? No matter though the fisherman himself may be coarse, and ragged, and rugged; yet he may light upon a priceless pearl.

And you, whoever you may be, I charge you in the name of the eternal God, plunge yourself into your work with whole-hearted devotion, and you shall yet discover some hidden jewel, which shall adorn Immanuel's diadem.

* * * * * *

DIVINE GOODNESS—Unceasing

It is by no means pleasant when reading an interesting article in your magazine to find yourself pulled up short with the ominous words, "to be continued." Yet they are words of good cheer if applied to other matters. What a comfort to remember that the Lord's mercy and loving-kindness is to be continued! Much as we have experienced in the long years of our pilgrimage, we have by no means outlived eternal love. Providential goodness is an endless chain, a stream which follows the pilgrim, a wheel perpetually revolving, a star for ever shining, and leading us to the place where he is who was once a babe in Bethlehem. All the volumes which record the doings of divine grace are but part of a series to be continued.

* * * * * *

DOCTRINES—Not For Controversy

"A huge fragment of rock from an adjacent cliff fell upon a horizontal part of the hill below, which was occupied by the gardens and vineyards of two peasants. It covered part of the property of each, nor could it be easily decided to whom the unexpected visitor belonged: but the honest rustics instead of troubling the gentlemen of the long robe with their dispute, wisely resolved to end it by each party excavating the half of the rock on his own grounds, and converting the whole into two useful cottages, with comfortable rooms, and cellars for their little stock of wine, and there they now reside with their families.

After such a sort will wise men deal with the great doctrines of the gospel; they will not make them the themes of angry controversy, but of profitable use. To fight over a doctrine is sorry waste of time, but to live in the quiet enjoyment of it is the truest wisdom."

* * * * * *

DOING—More

Never talk of what you have done, but go on to something else. An officer rode up to his general, and said, "Sir, we have taken two guns from the enemy." "It is well," said the general, "take two more."

* * * * * *

DOUBT—Cure For.

When a soul has drawn near to Jesus, and has been fed by Him, it is no more troubled with doubts than a man at the equator is bitten by frost. "I believe in the Bible," said one. "How can you do that?" sneered another. "Because I know the Author," was the fit reply. If you are walking in the light with your Lord, questions and doubts are heard no more but you adore in deep restfulness of soul, "knowing that it is the Lord."

* * * * * *

DUTY—Doing Your

The officers were after our Lord, and He knew it. He could spy them out in the crowd, but He was not therefore in the least afraid or disconcerted. He reminds me of that minister who, when he was about to preach, was stopped by a soldier, who held a pistol at his head and threatened that if he spake he would kill him. "Soldier," said he, "do your duty; I shall do mine"; and he went on with his preaching. The Saviour, without saying as much in words, said so by His actions.

* * * * * *

DWARFS—Spiritual

There was once in London a club of small men, whose qualification for membership lay in their not exceeding five feet in height; these dwarfs held, or pretended to hold, the opinion that they were nearer the perfection of manhood than others, for they argued that primeval men had been far more gigantic than the present race, and consequently that the way of progress was to grow less and less, and that the human race as it perfected itself would become as diminutive as themselves.

Such a club of Christians might be established in most cities, and without any difficulty might attain to an enormously numerous membership; for the notion is common that our dwarfish Christianity is, after all, the standard, and many even imagine that nobler Christians are enthusiasts, fanatical and hot-blooded, while they themselves are cool because they are wise, and indifferent because they are intelligent.

* * * * * *

EFFICACY—Of Earthy Prayer

A lady was one day at an evening party, and there met with Caesar Malan, the famous divine of Geneva, who, in his usual manner, enquired of her whether she was a Christian. She was startled, surprised and vexed, and made a short reply to the effect that it was not a question she cared to discuss; whereupon Mr. Malan replied with great sweetness that he would not persist in speaking of it, but he would pray that she might be led to give her heart to Christ, and become a useful worker for Him.

Within a fortnight she met the minister again and asked him how she must come to Jesus. Mr. Malan's reply was, "Come to Him just as you are." The lady gave herself up to Jesus: it was Charlotte Elliott, to whom we owe that precious hymn:

> Just as I am without one plea.
> But that Thy blood was shed for me,
> And that Thou bid'st me come to Thee,
>   O Lamb of God I come.

It was a blessed thing for her that she was at that party, and that the servant of God from Geneva should have been there, and should have spoken to her so faithfully.

* * * * * *

ENQUIRERS—Not to be Discouraged

At the Synod of Moscow, held by King Goutran, A.D. 585, bishops were forbidden to keep dogs in their houses, or birds of prey, lest the poor should be bitten by these animals instead of being fed. Should not all ministers be equally concerned to chase away all morose habits, angry tempers and repulsive manners, which might discourage the approach of enquiring souls who desire to know of us the way of salvation? Sunday-school teachers may also take the hint.

* * * * * *

EXAGGERATION

In certain ancient Italian frescoes, Mary Magdalene is drawn as a woman completely enveloped in her own hair, which reaches to her feet and entirely wraps up her body as in a seamless garment. These queer draughtsmen must needs exaggerate; granted that the woman had long hair, they must enfold her in it like a silkworm in its own silk.

The practice survives among the tribe of talkers, everything with them is on the enlarged scale; a man with ordinary abilities is a prodigy, another with very pardonable faults is a monster, and a third with a few failings is a disgrace to humanity. Truth is as comely and beautiful as a woman with flowing hair, but exaggeration is as grotesque and ugly as the Magdalene, all hair from head to foot.

* * * * * *

FAITH

It seemed almost a novelty in the church when it was stated, some years ago, that Mr. George Muller walked by faith in regard to temporal things. To feed children by faith in God was looked upon as a pious freak. We have come to a pretty pass, have we not, when God is not to be trusted about common things?

* * * * * *

FAITH

The Emperor Napoleon I was reviewing some troops upon the Place du Carrousel, in Paris; and, in giving an order, he thoughtlessly dropped the bridle upon his horse's neck, which instantly set off on a gallop. The emperor was obliged to cling to the saddle. At this moment a common soldier of the line sprang before the horse, seized the bridle, and handed it respectfully to the emperor. "Much obliged to you, captain," said the chief, by this one word making the soldier a captain. The man believed the emperor, and, saluting him, asked, "Of what regiment, Sire?" Napoleon, charmed with his faith, replied, "Of my guards!" and galloped off.

You now see how a person may be sure that God gives peace: it is by believing His testimony, just as this soldier believed that of his emperor. That is to say, as he believed himself to be a captain before wearing his uniform; so on the word and promise of God, one believes himself to be a child of Jesus before being sanctified by His Spirit.—*Caesar Malan, D.D.*

* * * * * *

FAITH—Overcoming Temptation

When a traveller was asked whether he did not admire the admirable structure of some stately building, "No," said he, "for I've been at Rome, where better are to be seen every day." O believer, if the world tempt thee with its rare sights and curious prospects, thou mayst well scorn them, having been, by contemplation, in heaven, and being able, by faith, to see infinitely better delights every hour of the day. "This is the victory which overcometh the world, even our faith."

* * * * * *

FAITH—Triumph of

During an earthquake that occurred a few years since, the inhabitants of a small village were generally very much alarmed, but they were at the same time surprised at the calmness and apparent joy of an old lady whom they all knew. At length one of them, addressing the old lady, said: "Mother, are you not afraid?" "No," said the mother in Israel; "I rejoice to know that I have a God that can shake the world."

* * * * * *

FEAR OF SIN

The old naturalist, Ulysses Androvaldus, tells us that a dove is so afraid of a hawk, that she will be frightened at the sight of one of its feathers. Whether it be so or not,

I cannot tell, but this I know, that when a man has had a thorough shaking over the jaws of hell, he will be so afraid of sin, that even one of its feathers—any one sin—will alarm and send a thrill of fear through his soul. This is a part of the way by which the Lord turns us when we are turned indeed.

* * * * * *

FLORAL PREACHING

Many are the floral displays in sermons. Sheaves of corn are too plain and rustic. This is the age of bouquets and wreaths of rare flowers. Paul must give way to Browning, and David to Tennyson. There are enough in the novelty business without us: and we have something better to do. We have to give an account unto our God of what we do and say, and if we have been murderers of souls, it will be no excuse that we flourished the dagger well, or that when we gave them poison we mixed the drought cleverly, and presented it with poetical phrases.

* * * * * *

FRIVOLITIES—Render Men Callous to the Gospel

"When Bonaparte put the Duke d'Enghien to death, all Paris felt so much horror at the event that the throne of the tyrant trembled under him. A counter-revolution was expected, and would most probably have taken place, had not Bonaparte ordered a new ballet to be brought out, with the utmost splendour, at the Opera. The subject he pitched on was 'Ossian, or the Bards.' It is still recollected in Paris, as perhaps the grandest spectacle that had ever been exhibited there. The consequence was that the murder of the Duke d'Enghien was totally forgotten, and nothing but the new ballet was talked of."

After this fashion Satan takes off men's thoughts from their sins, and drowns the din of their consciences. Lest they should rise in revolt against him, he gives them the lusts of the flesh, the vanities of pride, the cares of this world, or the merriment of fools, to lead away their thoughts. Poor silly men are ready enough for these misleading gaieties, and for the sake of them the solemnities of death and eternity are forgotten.

* * * * * *

GLORY TO GOD

When we get to heaven it will be, "Glory be to God for ever and ever and ever." We shall not hum even a single note to ourselves for our own glory or on account of any part of the work for which we deserved credit, but we shall ascribe the whole of our salvation to infinite love and undeserved favor, and to the unceasing faithfulness and power of our gracious covenant-keeping God.

* * * * * *

GOD LIVES

While God lives, truth is in the ascendant. I remember years ago meeting with that blessed servant of God, the late Earl of Shaftesbury. He was at Mentone with a dying daughter, and he happened that day to be very much downcast—as, indeed, I have frequently seen him, and as, I am sorry to confess, he has also frequently seen me.

That day he was particularly cast down about the general state of society. He thought that the powers of darkness in this country were having it all their own way, and that, before long, the worst elements of society would gain power, and trample out all virtue. Looking up into his face, I said to him, "And is God dead? Do you believe that while God lives the devil will conquer Him?"

He smiled, and we walked along by the Mediterranean communing together in a far more hopeful tone. The Lord liveth and blessed be my Rock. As long as the Lord liveth our hope lives also. Gospel truth will yet prevail; we shall live to see the old faith to the front again. The church, like Noah's dove, will come back to her nest again, and bring somewhat with her which shall prophesy eternal peace.

* * * * * *

GOD'S WORD—To be Believed

Locke, the great philosopher, spent the last fourteen years of his life in the study of the Bible, and when asked what was the shortest way for a young gentleman to understand the Christian religion, he bade him read the Bible, remarking: "Therein are contained the words of eternal life. It has God for its author, salvation for its end, and truth, without any admixture of error, for its matter." There are those on the side of God's Word whom you need not be ashamed of in the matter of intelligence and learning.

* * * * * *

GOD—With His Saints

As the heavens stand unshored and unsupported, save by the Word of God, so stands the man of God. Remember how Luther realized this; and when they said that Duke George would oppose him, he said, "If it rained Duke Georges, I would not care, so long as I have God with me."

* * * * * *

GOD—Unchanging

The Christian knows no change with regard to God. He may be rich today and poor tomorrow; he may be sickly today and well tomorrow; he may be in happiness today, tomorrow he may be distressed—but there is no change with regard to his relationship to God. If He loved me yesterday, He loves me today. My unmoving mansion of rest is my blessed Lord.

* * * * * *

GOSPEL—No Monopolizing the

I have heard say that in the old Bread Riots, when men were actually starving for bread, no word had such a terribly threatening and alarming power about it as the word "Bread!" when shouted by a starving crowd. I have read a description by one who once heard this cry: he said he had been startled at night by a cry of "Fire!" but when he heard the cry of "Bread!" "Bread!" from those who were hungry, it seemed to cut him like a sword. Whatever bread had been in his possession he must at once have handed it out. So it is with the gospel; when men are once aware of their need of it, there is no monopolizing it.

* * * * * *

GOSPEL—For Plain People

Some time ago a person who wanted, I suppose, to make me feel my own insignificance, wrote to say that he had met with a number of negroes who had read my sermons with evident pleasure, and he wrote that he believed they were very suitable for what he was pleased to call "niggers." Yes, my preaching was just the sort of stuff for niggers. The gentleman did not dream what sincere pleasure he caused me, for if I am understood by poor people, by servant-girls, by children, I am sure I can be understood by others.

* * * * * *

GOSPEL

If you stand half a mile off from a man and throw the Gospel at him you will miss him, but if you go close to him and lay hold upon him, giving him a hearty grip of the hand, and show that you have an affection for him, you will, by God's blessing, lead him in the right way.

* * * * * *

GOSPEL—Plain

A man said, about something he wished to make clear, "Why, it is as plain as A B C!" "Yes," said a third party, "but the man you are talking to is D E F." So some of our hearers seem to turn away from the Word of God. Let us explain the gospel as we may, if there is no desire in the heart, our plainest messages are lost.

* * * * * *

GOSPEL—Poor Man's

The longer I live, the more I bless God that we have not received a classical gospel, or a mathematical gospel, or a metaphysical gospel; it is not a gospel confined to scholars and men of genius, but a poor man's gospel, a ploughman's gospel; for that is the kind of gospel which we can live upon and die upon. It is to us not the luxury of refinement, but the staple food of life. We want no fine words when the heart is heavy, neither do we need deep problems when we are lying upon the verge of eternity, weak in body and tempted in mind. At such times we magnify the blessed simplicity of the gospel. Jesus in the flesh made manifest becomes our soul's bread. Jesus bleeding on the cross, a substitute for sinners, is our soul's drink. This is the gospel for babes, and strong men want no more.

* * * * * *

GOSPEL—The Simple

I was struck with what one said the other day of a certain preacher. The hearer was in deep concern of soul, and the minister preached a very pretty sermon indeed, decorated abundantly with word-painting. I scarcely know any brother who can paint so daintily as this good minister can; but this pour soul, under a sense of sin, said, "There is too much landscape, sir; I did not want landscape, I wanted salvation."

Dear friend, never crave word-painting when you attend a sermon; but crave Christ. You must have Christ to be your own by faith, or you are a lost man.

* * * * * *

GOSPEL—Needs Spiritual Ears to Appreciate It

Alphonse Karr heard a gardener ask his master permission to sleep for the future in the stable; "for," said he, "there is no possibility of sleeping in the chamber behind the greenhouse, sir; there are nightingales there which do nothing but guggle, and keep up a noise all the night." The sweetest sounds are but an annoyance to those who have no musical ear; doubtless the music of heaven would have no charms to carnal minds, certainly the joyful sound of the gospel is unappreciated so long as men's ears remain uncircumcised.

* * * * * *

GOSPEL—Weary of the

I have heard of a flower girl who sold violets in the street, and had to take those that remained home to her poor, miserable room, every night, till she said that she hated the smell of violets: she could not bear them, having got so accustomed to them. "That is strange," says one; yet that is how some of our gospel-hearers speak. I dread above anything that your nostrils should become so familiar with the sweet smell of the Rose of Sharon and the Lily of the Valley, that their fragrance should become nauseous to you.

* * * * * *

GRATITUDE

There is a very touching little story told of a poor woman with two children, who had not a bed for them to lie upon, and scarcely any clothes to cover them. In the depth of winter they were nearly frozen, and the mother took the door of a cellar off the hinges, and set it up before the corner where they crouched down to sleep, that some of the draught and cold might be kept from them. One of the children whispered to her, when she complained of how badly off they were, "Mother, what do those dear little children do who have no cellar door to put up in front of them?" Even there, you see, the little heart found cause for thankfulness.

* * * * * *

HABITS—Destructive Power of

The surgeon of a regiment in India relates the following incident:—"A soldier rushed into the tent, to inform me that one of his comrades was drowning in a pond close by, and nobody could attempt to save him in consequence of the dense weeds which covered the surface. On repairing to the spot, we found the poor fellow in his last struggle, manfully attempting to extricate himself from the meshes of rope-like grass that encircled his body; but, to all appearance, the more he laboured to escape, the more firmly they became coiled round his limbs. At last he sank, and the floating plants closed in, and left not a trace of the disaster.

After some delay, a raft was made, and we put off to the spot, and sinking a pole some twelve feet, a native dived, holding on by the stake, and brought the body to the surface. I shall never forget the expression of the dead man's face—the clenched teeth, and fearful distortion of the countenance, while coils of long trailing weeds clung round his body and limbs, the muscles of which stood out stiff and rigid, whilst his hands grasped thick masses, showing how bravely he had struggled for life."

This heart-rending picture is a terribly accurate representation of a man with a conscience alarmed by remorse, struggling with his sinful habits, but finding them too strong for him. Divine grace can save the wretch from his unhappy condition, but if he be destitute of that, his remorseful agonies will but make him more hopelessly the slave of his passions. Laocoon, in vain endeavoring to tear off the serpent's coils from himself and children, aptly portrays the long-enslaved sinner contending with sin in his own strength. "Can the Ethiopian change his skin, or the leopard his spots?"

* * * * * *

HAPPY—DYING

Mr. Rowland Hill used merrily to say when he got old that he hoped that they had not forgotten him. That is how he came to look at death; and he would go to some old woman if he could, and say, "Now, dear sister, if you go before I go, mind that you give my love to John Bunyan, and the other Johns. Tell them that Rowley is stopping behind a little while, but he is coming on as fast as he can."

Oh! it is a sweet thing gradually to melt away, and have the tenement gradually taken down, and yet not to feel any trouble about it, but to know that you are in the great Father's hands, and you shall wake up where old age and infirmities will all have passed away, and where, in everlasting youth, you shall behold the face of Him you love.

* * * * * *

HEARERS

Jedediah Buxton, the famous peasant, who could multiply nine figures by nine in his head, was once taken to see

Garrick act. When he went back to his own village, he was asked what he thought of the great actor and his doings. "Oh!" he said, "he did not know, he had only seen a little man strut about the stage, and repeat 7,956 words." Here was a want of the ability to appreciate what he saw, and the exercise of the reigning faculty to the exclusion of every other. Similarly our hearers, if destitute of the spiritual powers by which the gospel is discerned, fix their thoughts on our words, tones, gestures, or countenance, and make remarks upon us which from a spiritual point of view are utterly absurd. How futile are our endeavours without the Holy Spirit!

* * * * * *

HEART—Must be Renewed

A man may beat down the bitter fruit from an evil tree until he is weary; whilst the root abides in strength and vigor, the beating down of the present fruit will not hinder it from bringing forth more. This is the folly of some men; they set themselves with all earnestness and diligence against the appearing eruption of lust, but leaving the principle and root untouched, perhaps unsearched out, they make but little or no progress in this work of mortification. —*John Owen.*

* * * * * *

HEART—Will of God in the

I have heard of a famous king of Poland, who did brave deeds in his day, and confessed that he owed his excellent character to a secret habit he had formed. He was the son of a noble father, and he carried with him a miniature portrait of this father, and often looked upon it.

Whenever he went to battle he would look upon the picture of his father, and nerve himself to valor. When he sat in the council-chamber he would secretly look upon the image of his father, and behave himself right royally: for he said, "I will do nothing that can dishonor my father's name." Now, this is the grand thing for a Christian to do —to carry about with him the will of God in his heart, and then in every action to consult that will.

* * * * * *

HEAVEN

I remember a man, born blind, who loved our Lord most intensely, and he was wont to glory in this, that his eyes had been reserved for his Lord. Said he, "The first whom I shall ever see will be the Lord Jesus Christ. The first sight that greets my newly-opened eyes will be the Son of Man in His glory."

* * * * * *

HEAVEN—IN US

An old Scotchman was asked whether he expected to get to heaven. "Why, man, I live there," was his quaint reply. Let us all live in those spiritual things which are the essential features of heaven. Often go there, before you go to stay there.

It was said of an old Puritan that heaven was in him before he was in heaven. That is necessary for all of us; we must have heaven in us before we get into heaven. If we do not get to heaven before we die, we shall never get there afterwards.

* * * * * *

HOLY WATER

Holy water, indeed! a vile mixture, neither fit for man nor beast. You see this liquid virtue at the doors of all the churches ready for the brows of the faithful, but what is far more curious, you observe it in little pots placed for use in the cemeteries; and that the passer-by may give the dead a showery benediction, there are little sprinkling brushes in the pots with which to scatter the precious mixture. A mother's tears over her dead babe are far more in place than such foolery.

Holy water! bah! See how the rain pours down from yonder black cloud which has passed over the rugged crags of Pilatus; that sort of holy water is infinitely more likely to moisten the clay of the defunct, and bring plenteous blessing to the living, than all the hogsheads of aqueous fluid that priests ever mumbled over. Holy water, indeed! If there be such a thing, it trickles from the eye of penitence, bedews the cheek of gratitude, and falls upon the page of holy Scripture when the word is applied with power.

* * * * * *

HOPE—For Great Sinners

You remember what the Scotchwoman said to Rowland Hill when she stood looking at his face. He said, "Well, good woman, you have looked at me a long while. What are you looking at?" She said, "I was looking at the lines of your face." "Well, and what do you make of them?" said he. "I was thinking what an awful rascal you would have been, if you were not converted," was her unexpected answer. Now I think we might say the same of a good many; and if it be God's intent, He should get a glorious name for Himself. I see hope for big rascals, I see hope for great sinners.

* * * * * *

HUMILITY

"Of all trees, I observe, God hath chosen the vine, a low plant that creeps upon the helpful wall; of all beasts, the soft and patient lamb; of all fowls, the mild and guileless dove. Christ is the rose of the field, and the lily of the valley. When God appeared to Moses, it was not in the lofty cedar, nor the sturdy oak, not the spreading plane; but in a bush, a humble, slender, abject shrub; as if He would, by these elections, check the conceited arrogance of man."—*Owen Feltham.*

* * * * * *

HYPOCRISY—PRESENT AGE SUITABLE TO

There was an age of chivalry, when no craven courted knighthood, for it involved the hard blows, the dangerous wounds, the rough unhorsings, and the ungentle perils of the tournament; nay, these were but child's play: there were distant eastern fields, where Paynim warriors must be slain by valiant hands, and blood must flow in rivers from the Red-cross knights. Then men who lacked valor preferred their hawks and their jesters, and left heroes to court death and glory on the battlefield. This genial time of peace breeds carpet knights, who flourish their untried weapons, and bear the insignia of valor, without incurring its inconvenient toils.

* * * * * *

HYPOCRISY

Think what it will be to have it proven that you were godly for the sake of gain; that you were generous out of ostentation or zealous for love of praise; that you were careful in public to maintain a religious reputation, but that all the while everything was done for self and self only.

* * * * * *

HYPOCRITES

The raw material for a devil is an angel. The raw material for the son of perdition was an apostle; and the raw material for the most horrible of apostates is one who is almost a saint. I say no more than I mean, and than history can prove. There have usually been splendid traits of character about men who have been unfit to live.

* * * * * *

HYPOCRITES—Seeking Their Own Advantage

God is in the hypocrite's mouth, but the world is in his heart, which he expects to gain through his good reputation. I have read of one that offered his prince a great sum of money to have leave once or twice a day to come into his presence, and only say, "God save your Majesty!" The prince wondering at this large offer for so small a favor, asked him, "What advantage would this afford him?" "O sire," saith he, "this, though I have nothing else at your hands, will get me a name in the country for one who is a great favorite at court, and such an opinion will help me to more at the year's end, than it costs me for the purchase."

Thus some, by the name they get for great saints, advance their worldly interests, which lie at the bottom of all their profession.—*Gurnall.*

* * * * * *

INSIGNIFICANT SUBJECTS—Not Fit for the Pulpit

Carlyle in narrating an instance of the preservation of etiquette at the court of Louis XVI, while the mob were demanding entrance into his private apartments, and the empire was going to pieces, compares it to the house cricket still chirping amid the pealing of the trump of doom.

When trivial subjects are descanted upon from the pulpit, while souls are perishing for lack of knowledge, the same comparison may be used; as for instance, when a congregation is collected, and the preacher talks about the drying up of the Euphrates, or ventilates his pet theory for reconciling Moses and geology. Why cannot these things be kept for other assemblies? What can the man be at?

Nero fiddling over burning Rome is nothing to it! Even
the women knitting in front of the guillotine were not more
coolly cruel. We tolerate the cricket for his incongruous
chirp, but go to, thou silly trifler at the sacred desk, we
cannot frame excuse for thee, or have patience with thee.

* * * * * *

INFIDELS

Some persons have no hope, or only one of which they
might justly be ashamed. Ask many who deny the Scriptures what is their hope for the future. "I shall die like a
dog," says one. "When I'm dead there's an end of me."
If I had such a wretched hope as that, I certainly would
not go about the world proclaiming it. I should not think
of gathering a large congregation like this and saying to
you: "Brethren, rejoice with me, for we are all to die like
cats and dogs." It would never strike me as a matter to
be gloried in.

* * * * * *

INCONSISTENCY

Mark Antony once yoked two lions together, and drove
them through the streets of Rome, but no human skill can
ever yoke together the Lion of the Tribe of Judah and the
Lion of the Pit. I did see a man once trying to walk on
both sides of the street at one time, but he was undoubtedly
drunk; and when we see a man laboring day by day to walk
on both sides of the street, morally—in the shady side of
sin and the sunny side of holiness, or reeling in the evening,
at one time towards the bright lights of virtue, and anon
staggering back to sin in dark places, where no lamp is
shining—we say of him, "He is morally intoxicated," and
wisdom adds, "He is mad, and if the Great Physician heal
him not, his madness will bring him to destruction."

* * * * * *

JESUS—THE NAME

If there be one name sweeter than another in a believer's
ear it is the name of JESUS. Jesus! it is the name which
moves the harps of heaven to melody. Jesus! the life of all
our joys. If there be one name more charming, more
precious than another, it is this name. It is woven into the
very warp and woof of our psalmody. Many of our hymns
begin with it, and scarcely any that are good for anything
end without it. It is the sum total of all delights. It is the
music with which the bells of heaven ring; a song in a word;
an ocean for comprehension, although a drop for brevity;
a matchless oratorio in two syllables; a gathering up of the
hallelujahs of eternity in five letters.

* * * * * *

JESUS—ONLY

I recollect a story told of William Dawson, whom our
Wesleyan friends used to call Billy Dawson, one of the best
preachers who ever entered a pulpit. He once gave out as
his text, "Through this Man is preached unto you the for-
giveness of sins." When he had given out his text he
dropped down to the bottom of the pulpit, so that nothing
could be seen of him, only there was a voice heard saying,
"Not the man in the pulpit, he is out of sight, but the Man
in the Book. The Man described in the Book is the Man
through whom is preached unto you the remission of sins."
I put myself and you, and everybody else out of sight, and
I preach to you the remission of sins through Jesus only.
I would sing with the children, "Nothing but the blood of
Jesus." Shut your eyes to all things but the cross.

* * * * * *

JOY—AT FINDING SALVATION

We are told of some Turks, who have, upon the sight of
Mohamet's tomb, put out their eyes, that they might not

defile them, forsooth, with any common object, after they had been blessed with seeing one so sacred. I am sure many gracious souls there have been, who, by a prospect of heaven's glory set before the eye of their faith, have been so ravished by the sight, that they desired God even to seal up their eyes by death, with Simeon, who would not by his good-will have lived a day after that blessed hour in which his eyes had beheld the salvation of God.—*W. Gournall.*

* * * * * *

JOY OF OUR RELIGION—As an Evidence of Its Truth

"How I long for my bed! Not that I may sleep—I lie awake often and long! but to hold sweet communion with my God. What shall I render unto him for all his revelations and gifts to me? Were there no historical evidence of the truth of Christianity, were there no well-established miracles, still I should believe that the religion propagated by the fisherman of Galilee is Divine. The holy joys it brings to me must be from heaven. Do I write this boastingly, brother? Nay, it is with tears of humble gratitude that I tell of the goodness of the Lord."—Extract from a Private Letter from *Bapa Padmanji,* one of the Native Converts in India.

* * * * * *

JUDGMENT—Perverted

When a traveller is newly among the Alps, he is constantly deceived in his reckoning. One Englishman declared that he could climb the Righi in half an hour, but after several panting hours the summit was still ahead of him; yet when he made the boast, some of us who stood by were much of his mind—the ascent seemed so easy. This partly accounts for the mistakes men make in estimating eternal things: they have been too much used to molehills to be at home with mountains. Only familiarity with the sublimities of revelation can educate us to a comprehension of their heights and depths.

* * * * * *

LABORERS—ARE FEW

Let me tell you what you are like. It is a hot autumn day, and a man is reaping; the sweat pours from his face, as he bends to the task, and he fears that he will never get to the end of the field, and all the time you are pleasantly occupied leaning over a gate, and saying, "That is an uncommonly good laborer." Or perhaps instead of doing that, you are saying, "Why, he does not handle the sickle properly; I could show him a better way of reaping." But as you never attempt to show us, we have only your own word to go by, and you must excuse us being a little skeptical on the matter. The work of the church is generally left to a few earnest folk, is it not? Is that right?

* * * * * *

LIGHT—OUR JOY

A poor boy who was put down in the coal mines to close a door after the coal wagons had passed by, was forced to sit there alone, hour after hour, in the dark. He was a gracious child, and when one said to him. "Are you not weary with sitting so long in the dark?" he said, "Yes, I do get tired; but sometimes the men give me a bit of candle, and when I get a light, I sing." So do we; when we get a light we sing. Glory be to God, He is our light and our salvation, and therefore we sing. O child of God, when your eye is single, and the light of God fills every part of your being, then you sing, and sing again, and feel that you can never have done singing on earth till you begin singing in Heaven.

* * * * * *

LIFE OF THE BELIEVER—Interesting

I heard a gentleman assert that he could walk almost any number of miles when the scenery was good; but, he added, "When it is flat and uninteresting, how one tires!" What scenery enchants the Christian pilgrim; the towering mountains of predestination, the great sea of providence, the rocks of sure promise, the green fields of revelation, the river that makes glad the city of God, all these compose the scenery which surrounds the Christian, and at every step fresh sublimities meet his view.

* * * * * *

LIFE—Reviewed

Here is a good searching question for a man to ask himself as he reviews his past life: Have I written in the snow? Will my life-work endure the lapse of years and the fret of change? Has there been anything immortal in it, which will survive the speedy wreck of all sublunary things? The boys inscribe their names in capitals in the snow, and in the morning's thaw the writing disappears; will it be so with my work, or will the characters which I have carved outlast the brazen tablets of history? Have I written in the snow?

* * * * * *

LIFE—To be Viewed in Reference to its End

The way is good, says Chrysostom, if it be to a feast, though through a dark and miry lane; if to an execution not good, though through the fairest street of the city. Non qua sed quo. Not the way but the end is to be mainly considered.

* * * * * *

LIGHT—Detested by the Wicked

A sluttish housemaid, when scolded for the untidiness of the chambers, exclaimed, "I'm sure the rooms would be clean enough if it were not for the nasty sun which is always showing the dirty corners." Thus do men revile the gospel because it reveals their own sin. Thus all agitations for reforms in Church and State are opposed, and all manner of mischief attributed to them as if they created the evils which they bring to light. The lover of the right courts anything which may manifest the wrong, but those who love evil have never a good word for those disturbing beams of truth which show up the filthy corners of their hearts and lives.

* * * * * *

LUST

Our lusts are cords. Fiery trials are sent to burn and consume them. Who fears the flame which will bring him liberty from bonds intolerable?

* * * * * *

MEDITATION—To be Practised

Those who would be in health do not sit still in their houses to breathe such air as may come to them, but they walk abroad and seek out rural and elevated spots that they may inhale the invigorating breezes; and thus those godly souls who would be in a vigorous spiritual state, do not merely think upon such holy doctrines as may come into their minds in the ordinary course of thought, but they give time to meditation, they walk abroad in the fields of truth, and endeavor to climb the heights of gospel promises. It is said that Enoch walked with God: here is not an idle but an active communion. The road to bodily health is said to be a footpath, and the way to spiritual health is to exercise one's self in holy contemplation.

* * * * * *

MEN—CATCHING

I sometimes hear of persons getting very angry after a gospel sermon, and I say to myself, "I am not sorry for it." Sometimes when we are fishing the fish gets the hook into his mouth. He pulls hard at the line; if he were dead, he would not; but he is a live fish, worth the getting; and though he runs away for awhile, with the hook in his jaws, he cannot escape. His very wriggling and his anger show that he has got the hook, and the hook has got him. Have the landing-net ready; we shall land him by and by. Give him more line; let him spend his strength, and then we will land him, and he shall belong to Christ forever.

* * * * * *

MERCY—CONTINUAL

A benevolent person gave Mr. Rowland Hill a hundred pounds to dispense to a poor minister, and thinking it was too much to send him all at once, Mr. Hill forwarded five pounds in a letter, with simply these words within the envelope, "More to follow." In a few days' time, the good man received another letter by the post—letters by the post were rarities in those days; this second messenger contained another five pounds, with the same motto, "And more to follow." A day or two after came a third and a fourth, and still the same promise, "And more to follow." Till the whole sum had been received the astonished minister was made familiar with the cheering words, "And more to follow."

Every blessing that comes from God is sent with the self-same message, "And more to follow." "I forgive you

your sins, but there's more to follow." "I justify you in
the righteousness of Christ, but there's more to follow."
"I adopt you into my family, but there's more to follow."
"I educate you for heaven, but there's more to follow." "I
give you grace upon grace, but there's more to follow." "I
have helped you even to old age, but there's still more to
follow." "I will uphold you in the hour of death, and as
you are passing into the world of spirits, My mercy shall
still continue with you, and when you land in the world to
come there shall still be MORE TO FOLLOW."

* * * * * *

MINDING—EARTHLY THINGS

I have heard of a person who walked some seven hundred
miles to see the Niagara Falls. When he was within seven
miles of the Falls, he thought he heard the roar of the
cataract, and he called to a man working in the fields, and
said, "Is that the roar of Niagara?" The man said, "I don't
know, but I guess it may be. What if it is?" With surprise
the good man said, "Do you live here?" "Born and bred
here," the man answered. "And yet you don't know
whether that thundering noise is from the waterfall?" "No,
stranger, I have never seen those falls, I look after my
farm."

No doubt there are many within hail of heaven's choicest
joys who have never cared to know them. They hope they
are saved, but they don't care for great joy. They dig
their potatoes. They use their spade and their hoe; but the
Niagara is nought to them. Many look well to this life, but
do not arouse themselves to gain present spiritual joy.

* * * * * *

MINISTER

However learned, godly and eloquent a minister may be,
he is nothing without the Holy Spirit. The bell in the

steeple may be well hung, fairly fashioned, and of soundest metal, but it is dumb until the ringer makes it speak; and in like manner the preacher has no voice of quickening for the dead in sin, or of comfort for living saints until the divine Spirit gives him a gracious pull, and bids him speak with power. Hence the need of prayer from both preacher and hearers.

* * * * * *

MINISTER—Self-dissatisfaction of

> "Swift of foot was Hiawatha,
> He could shoot an arrow from him,
> And run forward with such fleetness,
> That the arrow fell behind him!"

The fable is even less than truth with the fervent preacher: he darts arrows of fire in flaming speech, but his eagerness to win souls far outruns his words. He projects himself far beyond his language. His heart outstrips his utterance. He embraces souls in his love, while his words as yet are but on the wing. Often and often will he weep when his sermon is over, because his words "fell behind him"; yet has he cause for joy, that he should have received so divine a spirit from his Master's hand: his very dissatisfaction proves his zeal.

* * * * * *

MISUNDERSTOOD

I have heard of a man who lived in a certain town, and while he lived was greatly misunderstood. It was known that he had a large income, yet he lived a miserly life, and loud were the murmurs at the scanty help he gave to those around him. He stinted in many ways, and hoarded his money. But when he died, the popular verdict was reversed, for then the motive of all his economy was manifested. He left his fortune to build a reservoir and an aqueduct, to bring a constant supply of water to the town where he had been despised and misunderstood.

This was the chief need of the people, and for a long time they had suffered much from drought and disease, because of the scanty supply. All the years that they had misjudged him, he was silently, unselfishly living for their sakes; when they discovered his motive, it was too late to do anything for him further than to hand down to future generations the memory of his noble and generous deed. But we can do much "for His sake," who has brought to us the living water; and who, though He died for us, is now alive again, and will live forevermore.

* * * * * *

MODELS—Should be Perfect

A great painter once had finished a picture, and he said to his wife, with tears in his eyes, "It is all over with me, I shall never paint again, I am a ruined man." She enquired, "Why?" "Because," he says, "that painting contents and satisfies me; it realized my idea of what painting ought to be, and therefore, I am sure my power is gone."

* * * * * *

MONEY-MAKING—No Time for

A gentleman of Boston, an intimate friend of Professor Agassiz, once expressed his wonder that a man of such abilities as he (Agassiz) possessed should remain contented with such a moderate income. "I have enough," was Agassiz's reply. "I have not time to make money. Life is not sufficiently long to enable a man to get rich, and do his duty to his fellow men at the same time." Christian, have you time to serve your God and yet to give your whole soul to gaining wealth? The question is left for conscience to answer.

* * * * * *

MORALIST

The dahlia would surely be a very empress among flowers if it had but perfume equal to its beauty; even the rose might need to look to her sovereignty. Florists have tried all their arts to scent this lovely child of autumn but in vain, no fragrance can be developed or produced; God has denied the boon, and human skill cannot impart it.

The reflecting mind will be reminded of those admirable characters which are occasionally met with, in which everything of good repute and comely aspect may be seen, but true religion, that sweet ethereal perfume of grace, is wanting; if they had but love to God, what lovely beings they would be, the best of the saints would not excel them, and yet that fragrant grace they do not seek, and after every effort we may make for their conversion, they remain content without the one thing which is needful for their perfection. O that the Lord would impart to them the mystic sweetness of His grace by the Holy Spirit!

* * * * * *

MORALITY A CURSE

When young men see an excellent person like you, so moral and amiable, without religion, they gather from your example that godliness is not absolutely needful, and take license to do without it. Thus you may be a curse where you little suspect it; you may be encouraging others in the attempt to live without the Savior.

* * * * * *

MOTHER

Here is a little child picked from the gutter; it is starved, unclothed, unwashed, and sickening to death. What does it want? Well, it would take me a long time to write out a list of all its wants. It needs washing, clothing, warming, feeding, nursing, loving—no, I will not attempt to complete the catalogue, but I will tell you all in a word; this little child wants its mother. If it finds a loving and capable mother, it has all that it needs at once. Every lost soul of man needs a thousand things; but no soul needs more than it will find in God.

* * * * * *

NEW CREATURES

I remember reading a famous writer's description of a wretched cab-horse which was old and worn out, and yet kept on its regular round of toil. They never took him out of harness for fear they should never be able to get his poor old carcass into it again. He had been in the shafts for so many years that they feared if they took him out of them he would fall to pieces, and so they let him keep where he was accustomed to be.

Some men are just like that. They have been in the shafts of sin so many years that they fancy that if they were once to alter they would drop to pieces. But it is not so, old friend. We are persuaded better things of you, and things that accompany salvation. The Lord will make a new creature of you. When He cuts the traces and brings you out from between those shafts which have so long held you, you will not know yourself.

* * * * * *

OPPOSITION—Helpful

Many, many years ago, a number of persons were seen to be going towards Smithfield, early one morning, and somebody said, "Whither are you going?" "We are going to Smithfield." "What for?" "To see our pastor burnt."

"Well, but what in the name of goodness do you want to see him burnt for? What can be the good of it?" They answered, "We are going to see him burn, to learn the way."

Oh, but that was grand. "To learn the way." Then the rank and file of the followers of Jesus learned the way to suffer and die as the leaders of the church set the example. Yet the church in England was not destroyed by persecution, but is become more mighty than ever, because of the opposition of its foes.

* * * * * *

OBEYING GOD—With Delight

"I wish I could mind God as my little dog minds me," said a little boy, looking thoughtfully on his shaggy friend; "he always looks so pleased to mind and I don't." What a painful truth did this child speak! Shall the poor little dog thus readily obey his master, and we rebel against God, who is our Creator, our Preserver, our Father, our Savior, and the bountiful Giver of everything we love?—*Christian Treasury.*

* * * * * *

OMNISCIENCE

A plate of sweet cakes was brought in and laid upon the table. Two children played upon the hearthrug before the fire. "Oh, I want one of these cakes!" cried the little boy, jumping up as soon as his mother went out, and going on tiptoe towards the table. "No, no," said his sister, pulling him back; "no, no; you must not touch." "Mother won't know it; she did not count them," he cried, shaking her off, and stretching out his hand. "If she didn't perhaps God counted," answered the other. The little boy's hand was stayed. Yes, children, be sure that God counts!—*Children's Missionary Record for 1852.*

* * * * * *

PARDON—Free

A prisoner was taken out to die, and as he rode along in the death-cart his heart was heavy at the thought of death, and none could cheer him of all the throng. The gallows-tree was in sight, and this blotted out the sun from him. But lo, his prince came riding up in hot haste bearing a free pardon. Then the man opened his eyes, and, as though he had risen from the dead, he returned to happy consciousness. The sight of his prince had chased all gloom away. He declared that he had never seen a fairer countenance in all his days: and when he read his pardon he vowed that no poetry should ever be dearer to his heart than those few lines of sovereign grace. Friends, I remember well when I was in that death-cart, and Jesus came to me with pardon.

* * * * * *

PEACE—Made With God

I like the language of a poor bricklayer, who fell from a scaffold, and was so injured that he was ready to die. The clergyman of the parish came and said, "My dear man, I am afraid you will die. You had better make your peace with God." To the joy of the clergyman, the man said, "Make my peace with God, sir! That was made for me upon Calvary's Cross eighteen hundred years ago; and I know it." Ah! that is it—to have peace that was made by the blood of Christ all those years ago—a peace that can never be broken. Then come life, come death, aye! come a lengthened life and ripe old age: the best preparation for a lengthened life is to know the Lord.

* * * * * *

PERSECUTION

I was reading the other day the life of John Philpot, who was shut up in Bishop Bonner's coal-hole in Fulham Palace.

There he and his friends sang psalms so merrily that the
Bishop chided them for their mirth. They could have
quoted apostolical authority for singing in prison. When
there were seven of them, Philpot wrote: "I was carried to
my lord's coal-house again, where I, with my six fellow
prisoners, do rouse together in the straw as cheerfully, we
thank God, as others do in their beds of down."

To be with the people of God, one would not mind being
in the coal-hole. No one wants to be in Bonner's coal-hole;
but better be there with the martyrs than upstairs in the
palace with the Bishop. To hear the saints' holy talk, and
sing with them their gladsome psalms, and with them behold
the angel of the covenant, is a very different thing from
mere suffering or imprisonment.

* * * * * *

PERSECUTION

The cold water of persecution is often thrown on the
church's face to fetch her to herself when she is in a swoon
of indolence or pride.

* * * * * *

PERSECUTION—NOT TO BE FEARED

Do not fear the frown of the world. When a blind man
comes against you in the street you are not angry at him.
You say, "He is blind, poor man, or he would not have
hurt me." So you may say of the poor worldlings when
they speak evil of Christians—they are blind.—*M'Cheyne*.

* * * * * *

PETITIONING GOD

The heart must be set upon its design. See how a child
cries! Though I am not fond of hearing it, yet I note that
some children cry all over; when they want a thing, they

cry from the tips of their toes to the last hair of their heads. That is the way to preach, and that is the way to pray, and that is the way to live; the whole man must be heartily engaged in holy work.

* * * * * *

PERSEVERANCE

I am reminded of Sir Christopher Wren, when he cleared away old St. Paul's to make room for his splendid pile. He was compelled to use battering-rams upon the massive walls. The workmen kept on battering and battering. An enormous force was brought to bear upon the walls for days and nights, but it did not appear to have made the least impression upon the ancient masonry.

Yet the great architect knew what he was at: he bade them keep on incessantly, and the ram fell again and again upon the rocky wall, till at length the whole mass was disintegrating and coming apart; and then each stroke began to tell. At a blow it reeled, at another it quivered, at another it moved visibly, at another it fell over amid clouds of dust. These last strokes did the work. Do you think so? No, it was the combination of blows, the first as truly as the last. Keep on with the battering-ram.

* * * * * *

POPERY

Lightfoot observes: "Yoke-fellows, indeed, are the Jew and Romanist above all people of the world, in a deluded fancying their own bravery and privilege above all the world besides. He that comes to read the Jewish writings, especially those that are of the nature of sermons, will find this to be the main stuffing of them, almost in every leaf and page. 'How choice a people is Israel! how dearly God is in love with Israel! what a happy thing it is to be of the seed of Abraham! how blessed the nation of the Jews above all nations!' And such stuff as this all along.

"And is not the style of the Romanists the very same tune? 'How holy the Church of Rome! what superiority and pre-eminence hath the church above all churches, and all the men in the world are heretics, and apostates, and cast-aways, if they be not Romanists.' Whereas if both these people would but impartially look upon themselves, they would see that there are such brands upon them as are upon no nation under heaven now extant."

* * * * * *

POWER OF TRUTH

A Unitarian minister who preached that wild doctrine of universal salvation, which is so popular just now, once met an old fashioned Baptist brother, who was not a well educated man, but who had a crowded congregation, while his brother had only a dozen or two to hear him eloquently discourse.

The Unitarian said, "I cannot make out how it is that there is such a difference in our congregations, you get so many to hear you, and I so few. I preach a very pleasing doctrine. I tell the people that all will be right with them at last. I do not worry them with any doctrines of repentance and faith and atonement, and yet they will not come to hear me. You preach a very dreary doctrine, and you tell the people that except they repent they shall perish and be cast into hell, and yet they crowd your place to hear you. How is that?"

"Well," said the old man, "I think it is, my friend, because they have a shrewd suspicion that what I say is true, and that what you say is not true." There he hit the nail on the head. It is so. The conscience of men bids them

distrust the word which tells them there will be no difference between the righteous and the wicked.

* * * * * *

PRAYER—Prevalent

Those who deny the efficacy of prayer never pray; nay,
are not capable of offering prevalent prayer. Yet these
fellows get up and say it is of no avail. They remind me of
the Irish prisoner who was brought up for murder, and
half a dozen people swore that they had seen him do the
deed. "Your lordship," said he, "I could bring you ten
times as many who didn't see me do it." Yes, but that was
no evidence at all; and in the same way these people have
the impudence to set up their theory on no better grounds
than the fact that they do not pray and God does not hear
them.

* * * * * *

PRAYER—For Help to Pray

In Dr. Ryland's memoir of Andrew Fuller is the following anecdote. At a conference at Soham, a friend of
slender abilities being asked to pray, knelt down, and Mr.
Fuller and the company with him, when he found himself
so embarrassed, that, whispering to Mr. Fuller, he said, "I
do not know how to go on." Mr. F. replied in a whisper,
"Tell the Lord so." The rest of the company did not hear
what passed between them, but the man taking Mr. Fuller's
advice began to confess his not knowing how to pray as he
ought to pray, begging to be taught to pray, and so pro-
ceeded in prayer to the satisfaction of all the company.

* * * * * *

PREACHERS — To be Acquainted With Human
Nature

Michael Angelo, when painting an altar-piece in the con-
ventual church, in Florence, in order that the figures might

be as deathlike as possible, obtained permission of the prior to have the coffins of the newly-buried opened and placed beside him during the night;—an appalling expedient, but successful in enabling him to reproduce with terrible effect, not the mortal pallor only, but the very anatomy of death.

If we would preach well to the souls of men we must acquaint ourselves with their ruined state, must have their case always on our hearts both by night and day, must know the terrors of the Lord and the value of the soul, and feel a sacred sympathy with perishing sinners. There is no masterly, prevailing preaching without this.

* * * * *

PREACHERS—DIFFERENT

Those that are all in exhortation, no whit in doctrine, are like to them that snuff the lamp, but pour not in oil. Again, those that are all in doctrine, nothing in exhortation, drown the wick in oil, but light it not; making it fit for use if it had fire put to it, but as it is, rather capable of good than profitable for the present. Doctrine without exhortation makes men all brain, no heart; exhortation without doctrine makes the heart full, leaves the brain empty. Both together make a man. One makes a wise man, the other good; one serves that we may know our duty, the other that we may perform it. I will labor in both, but I know not in whether more. Men cannot practice unless they know; and they know in vain if they practice not.—*Bishop Hall.*

* * * * *

PREDESTINATION

They that talk of nothing but predestination, and will not proceed in the way of heaven till they be satisfied on that point, do as a man that would not come to London, unless at his first step he might set his foot upon the top of St. Paul's.—*The Table Talk of John Selden.*

* * * * * *

PREJUDICE—Ears Stopped with

I have read that in the reign of Queen Elizabeth there was a law made that everybody should go to his parish church; but many sincere Romanists loathed to go and hear Protestant doctrine. Through fear of persecution, they attended the parish church; but they took care to fill their ears with wool, so that they should not hear what their priests condemned. It is wretched work preaching to a congregation whose ears are stopped with prejudices.

* * * * * *

PRIDE—In Dictating to God

The petty sovereign of an insignificant tribe in North America every morning stalks out of his hovel, bids the sun good-morrow, and points out to him with his finger the course he is to take for the day. Is this arrogance more contemptible than ours when we would dictate to God the course of His providence, and summon Him to our bar for His dealings with us? How ridiculous does man appear when he attempts to argue with his God!

* * * * * *

PROVIDENCE—Special

When Master Bunyan was a lad, he was so foolhardy that when an adder rose against him, he took it in his hand and plucked the sting out of its mouth, but he was not harmed. It was his turn to stand sentinel at the siege of Nottingham, and as he was going forth, another man offered to take his place. That man was shot, and Master Bunyan thus escaped. We should have had no "Pilgrim's Progress" if it had not been for that. Did not God preserve him on purpose that he might be saved?

There are special interpositions of divine providence by which God spares ungodly men, whom He might have cut down long ago as cumbers of the ground: should we not look upon these as having the intention that the barren tree may be cared for yet another year, if haply it may bring forth fruit?

* * * * * *

PROCRASTINATION

Be not like the foolish drunkard who, staggering home one night, saw his candle lit for him. "Two candles!" said he, for his drunkenness made him see double, "I will blow out one," and as he blew it out, in a moment he was in the dark. Many a man sees double through the drunkenness of sin; he has one life to sow his wild oats in, and then he half expects another in which to turn to God; so, like a fool, he blows out the only candle that he has, and in the dark he will have to lie down forever. Haste thee, traveller, thou hast but one sun, and after that sets, thou wilt never reach thy home. God help thee to make haste now!

* * * * * *

VAIN PHILOSOPHY

Young men have flung away all hope of salvation in order that they might be thought to be men of culture; they have abjured faith in order to be esteemed "free-thinkers" by those whose opinions were not worth a pin's head. I charge you, dear friend, if you are beginning at all to be a slave of other people, break these wretched and degrading bonds.

* * * * * *

SHAM PROFESSORS

What numbers of professors I have known who go into one place of worship and hear one form of doctrine and

apparently approve it because the preacher is "a clever
man!" They hear an opposite teaching, and they are
equally at home, because again it is "a clever man!" They
join with a church, and you ask them, "Do you agree with
the views of that community?" They neither know nor
care what those views may be; one doctrine is as good as
another to them.

Their spiritual appetite can enjoy soap as well as butter;
they can digest bricks as well as bread. These religious
ostriches have a marvelous power of swallowing everything;
they have no spiritual discernment, no appreciation of truth.
They follow any "clever" person, and in this prove that they
are not the sheep of our Lord's pasture.

* * * * * *

PROFESSORS—Shells and Shams

I often see upon a sunny wall a chrysalis, and when I go
to take it down I find that the summer's sun has shone upon
it and the insect has developed, and left nothing but an
empty case behind. How often in the pew we find the
chrysalis of a man, but where is the man himself? Wait
till tomorrow morning, and see him in his shop; there is the
man; or to follow up the figure, there is the butterfly with all
its wings. Wait till you find our friend engaged in secular
employment to his own advantage, and then you will see
what he is made of; but in the work of the Lord he is not
worth his salt.

* * * * * *

PROFESSORS AND THEIR PROPS

So many people have a "lean to" religion. If their minister, or some other leading person, were taken away, their
back wall would be gone, and they would come to the
ground. In some cases the wife and mother, or the husband
and father, or the friend and teacher, constitute the main

support of the individual's religion; he leans upon others, and if these fail him there is an end of his hope.

* * * * * *

PLEASING GOD

Have you a friend to whom you wish to make a present? I know what you do—you try to find out what that friend would value, for you say, "I should like to give him what would please him." Do you want to give God something that is sure to please Him? You need not build a church of matchless architecture; I do not know that God cares much about stones and wood. You need not wait till you shall have amassed money to endow a row of almshouses. It is well to bless the poor, but Jesus said that one who gave two mites, which made a farthing, gave more than all the rich men who cast in of their wealth into the treasury. What would God my Father like me to give? He answers, "My son, give Me thine heart." He will be pleased with that, for He Himself seeks the gift.

* * * * * *

PROMPTNESS—In Doing Good

Quick must be the hand if an impression is to be made upon the melted wax. Once let the wax cool and you will press the seal in vain. Cold and hard it will be in a few moments, therefore let the work be quickly done. When men's hearts are melted under the preaching of the Word, or by sickness, or the loss of friends, believers should be very eager to stamp the truth upon the prepared mind. Such opportunities are to be seized with holy eagerness. Reader, do you know of such? If you be a lover of the Lord Jesus, hasten with the seal before the wax is cool.

* * * * * *

PROSPERITY—Evils of

Too long a period of fair weather in the Italian valleys creates such a superabundance of dust that the traveller sighs for a shower. He is smothered, his clothes are white, his eyes smart, the grit even grates between his teeth and finds its way down his throat; welcome are the rain clouds, as they promise to abate the nuisance.

Prosperity long continued breeds a plague of dust even more injurious, for it almost blinds the spirit and insinuates itself into the soul; a shower or two of grief proves a mighty blessing, for it deprives the things of earth of somewhat of their smothering power. A Christian making money fast is just a man in a cloud of dust; it will fill his eyes if he be not careful. A Christian full of worldly care is in the same condition, and had need look to it lest he be choked with earth. Afflictions might almost be prayed for if we never had them, even as in long stretches of fair weather men beg for rain to lay the dust.

* * * * * *

PROVIDENCE—Rightly Places Us

Suppose the mole should cry, "How I could have honored the Creator had I been allowed to fly." It would be very foolish, for a mole flying would be a most ridiculous object; while a mole fashioning its tunnels and casting up its castles, is viewed with admiring wonder by the naturalist, who perceives its remarkable suitability to its sphere.

The fish of the sea might say, "How could I display the wisdom of God if I could sing, or mount a tree, like a bird"; but a dolphin in a tree would be a very grotesque affair, and there would be no wisdom of God to admire in trouts singing in the groves; but when the fish cuts the wave with agile fin, all who have observed it say how wonderfully it

is adapted to its habitat, how exactly its every bone is
fitted for its mode of life.

Brother, it is just so with you. If you begin to say, "I
cannot glorify God where I am, and as I am," I answer,
neither could you anywhere if not where you are. Providence, which arranged your surroundings, appointed them
so that, all things being considered, you are in the position
in which you can best display the wisdom and the grace of
God.

* * * * * *

PULPIT

Clemens Brentano, a literary acquaintance of Dr.
Krummacher, and a Catholic, once said to the doctor, "Till
you Protestants pull down the chatter-box," ("Plapperkasten") he meant the pulpit, "or, at least, throw it into
the corner, where it ought to be, there is no hope of you."
I could only reply to him, "It is true indeed, that our
'Plapperkasten' stands greatly in the way of you Catholics."

The pulpit is the Thermopylae of Protestantism, the
tower of the flock, the Palladium of the church of God.
Well might Paul magnify his office, for not only Glasgow
but the city of our God "flourishes by the preaching of the
Word."

* * * * * *

PROMISES OF GOD

No promise is of private interpretation. Whatever God
has said to any one saint He has said to all. When He
opens a well for one it is that all may drink. When He
openeth a granary door to give out food, there may be
some one starving man who is the occasion of its being
opened, but all hungry saints may come and feed too.

* * * * * *

PURPOSE—UNITY OF

When writing a paper for the Natural History Society upon the habits of the wild pigeon, Audubon says, "So absorbed was my whole soul and spirit in the work, that I felt as if I were in the woods of America, among the pigeons, and my ears were filled with the sound of their rustling wings." We should all write, speak, and preach for our Lord Jesus far more powerfully if our love to the Lord were a passion so dominant as to make the great realities of eternity vividly real and supremely commanding in our minds.

* * * * * *

QUIETNESS—OF MIND

A Martyr was fastened to the stake, and the sheriff who was to execute him expressed his sorrow that he should persevere in his opinions, and compel him to set fire to the pile. The martyr answered, "Do not trouble yourself, for I am not troubling myself. Come and lay your hand upon my heart, and see if it does not beat quietly." His request was complied with, and he was found to be quite calm. "Now," said he, "lay your hand on your own heart, and see if you are not more troubled than I am; and then go your way, and, instead of pitying me, pity yourself!" When we have done right we need no man's pity, however painful the immediate consequences.

* * * * * *

QUESTIONS—FOOLISH THEOLOGICAL

The follies of the schoolmen should be a warning to all those who would mingle metaphysical speculations or prophetical theories with the simple doctrines of the Bible. There was among those learned men such a rage for Aristotle, that his ethics were frequently read to the people instead of the gospel, and the teachers themselves were employed either in wresting the words of Scripture to support the most monstrous opinions, or in discussing the most trivial questions.

To leave the consideration of well-known and soul-saving truths to fight over unimportant subtleties, is to turn our cornfields into poppy gardens. To imagine that the writers of unintelligible mysticism are men of great depth, is to find wisdom in the hootings of owls. True spirituality shuns the obscure and the dilettanti, and delights in the plain and practical; but there is much to fascinate in the superfine shams of the hour. Quintilian justly observes that the obscurity of an author is generally in proportion to his incapacity.

It is a most fitting thing to be looking for the coming of the Lord, but a most miserable waste of time to be spinning theories about it, and allowing the millions around us to perish in their sins.

* * * * * *

REASON AND FAITH

An old writer says:—Faith and Reason may be compared to two travellers: Faith is like a man in full health, who can walk his twenty or thirty miles at a time without suffering; Reason is like a child, who can only, with difficulty, accomplish three or four miles. "Well," says this old writer, "on a given day Reason says to Faith, 'O good Faith, let me walk with thee.' Faith replies, 'O Reason, thou canst never walk with me!' However, to try their paces, they set out together, but they soon find it hard to keep company. When they come to a deep river, Reason says, 'I can never ford this,' but Faith wades through it singing. When they reach a lofty mountain, there is the same exclamation of despair; and in such cases, Faith, in order not to leave Reason behind, is obliged to carry him on his back; and," adds the writer, "oh! what a luggage is Reason to Faith!"

* * * * * *

RECOGNITION—In Heaven

I cannot forget old John Ryland's answer to his wife: "John," she said, "will you know me in heaven?" "Betty," he replied, "I have known you well here, and I shall not be a bigger fool in heaven than I am now; therefore I shall certainly know you there." That seems to be clear enough.

We read in the New Testament, "They shall sit down with Abraham, Isaac and Jacob in the kingdom of heaven"; not sit down with three unknown individuals in iron masks, or three impersonalities who make part of the great PAN, nor three spirits who are exactly alike as pins made in a factory; but Abraham, Isaac and Jacob.

* * * * * *

RELIGIOUS ROUTINE

I have heard of soldiers sleeping while on the march, and I have known some good people to sleep while praying, till I have thought that their prayers were a kind of pious snore. They go on with the old phrases without considering what they mean by them. They are like crickets, whose notes are ever the same. "I sleep," says the spouse, "but my heart waketh"; but these might more truly say, "I do not sleep, and yet my heart is not awake."

Many prayers are like a grocer's or draper's account: Ditto, ditto, ditto. The petitions are as per usual. It is dreary when we have the shell of a prayer before us, but have no oyster in it. The brother's lips are here in prayer, but his soul has gone home to his shop, or to his farm. The sails of his mill go round as the wind blows, but he is not grinding anything, there is no grist in the mill, no intelligent loving desire. Let us get out of the ruts of phrases and set petitions. Mere routine religion is hateful, and yet how easily we fall into it. Let us not rest on our oars, and hope to make progress by the impetus already gained.

* * * * * *

RESTLESS MINDS

A mind on wheels knows no rest; it is as a rolling thing before the tempest. Struggle against the desire for novelty, or it will lead you astray as the will-o'-the-wisp deceives the traveller. If you desire to be useful, if you long to honor God, if you wish to be happy, be established in the truth, and be not carried about by every wind of doctrine in these evil days, "be ye steadfast, unmovable."

* * * * * *

REPROOFS—To Be Given in Love

Preaching on John XIII:14—the duty of disciples to wash one another's feet—Mr. Finlayson, of Helmsdale, observed, "One way in which disciples wash one another's feet is by reproving one another. But the reproof must not be couched in angry words, so as to destroy the effect; nor in tame, so as to fail of effect. Just as in washing a brother's feet, you must not use boiling water to scald, nor frozen water to freeze them."

* * * * * *

RESPONSIBILITY

John Brown, of Haddington, said to a young minister, who complained of the smallness of his congregation, "It is as large a one as you will want to give account for in the day of judgment." The admonition is appropriate, not to ministers alone, but to all teachers.

* * * * * *

REVIVAL—Absence and Presence of

The decline of a revival is a great testing season. It discovers the true believers by chilling the false. A frosty night or two suffices to nip all the exotic plants of a garden; but the hardy shrubs, the true natives of the soil, live on even in the severest cold. Converts raised in the hot-bed of excitement soon droop and die if the spiritual temperature of the church falls below summer heat: what are these worth compared with the hardy children of divine grace, whose inward life will continue in enduring vigor when all around is dead!

Yet we do not desire to see the revival spirit droop among us, for even the evergreens of our garden delight in a warmer season, for then they send forth their shoots and clothe themselves with new leaves; and thus it will be seen that the best of the saints are all the better for the holy glow of the "times of refreshing."

* * * * * *

RICHES THAT LAST

If a man should labor to be rich after the African fashion, and should accumulate a large store of shells and beads, when he came home to England he would be a beggar, even though he had a ship-load of such rubbish. So he who gives his heart and soul to the accumulation of gold and silver coin is a beggar when he comes into the spiritual realm, where such round medals are reckoned as mere forms of earth, non-current in heaven, and of less value than the least of spiritual blessings.

* * * * * *

RICHES—RUINED BY

Do not be over-anxious about riches. Get as much of true wisdom and goodness as you can; but be satisfied with a very moderate portion of this world's good. Riches may prove a curse as well as a blessing.

I was walking through an orchard, looking about me, when I saw a low tree laden more heavily with fruit than the rest. On a nearer examination, it appeared that the tree had been dragged to the very earth, and broken by the weight of its treasures. "Oh!" said I, gazing on the tree, "here lies one who has been ruined by his riches."

In another part of my walk, I came up with a shepherd, who was lamenting the loss of a sheep that lay mangled and dead at his feet. On enquiry about the matter, he told me that a strange dog had attacked the flock, that the rest of the sheep had got away through a hole in the hedge, but that the ram now dead had more wool on his back, than the rest, and the thorns of the hedge held him fast till the dog had worried him. "Here is another," said I, "Ruined by his riches."

When I see so many rich people, as I do, caring so much for their bodies, and so little for their souls, I pity them from the bottom of my heart, and sometimes think there are as many ruined by riches as by poverty.

* * * * * *

RISING IN THE WORLD—AMBITION FOR

Ambition, a good enough thing within reasonable bounds, is a very Apollyon among men, when it gets the mastery over them. Have you ever seen boys climbing a greasy pole to reach a hat or a handkerchief? If so, you will have noticed that the aspiring youths for the most part adopt plans and tricks quite as slimy as the pole; one covers his hands with sand, another twists a knotted cord, and scarcely one climbs fairly, and he is the one boy whose chance is smallest.

* * * * * *

SALVATION—NEVER TAKE FOR GRANTED

Perhaps you have almost taken it for granted that you love Jesus; but it must not be taken for granted. Some of you have been born in a religious atmosphere, you have lived in the midst of godly people, and you have never been out into the wicked world to be tempted by its follies; therefore you come to an immediate conclusion that you must assuredly love the Lord. This is unwise and perilous. I would have you fully assured of your love to Jesus, but I would not have you deceived by a belief that you love Him if you do not. Lord, search us and try us!

* * * * * *

SALVATION—MANY STEPS IN ONE

I am not going to say which is first, the new birth or faith or repentance. Nobody can tell which spoke of a wheel moves first; it moves as a whole. The moment the divine life comes into the heart we believe; the moment we believe the eternal life is there. We repent because we believe and believe while we repent.

* * * * * *

SCRIPTURES—READING OF

Lord Bacon tells of a certain bishop who used to bathe regularly twice every day, and on being asked why he bathed thus often, replied, "Because I cannot conveniently do it three times." If those who love the Scriptures were asked why they read the Bible so often, they might honestly reply, "because we cannot find time to read it oftener." The Appetite for the Word grows on that which it feeds on. We would say with Thomas á Kempis, "I would be always in a nook with a book."

* * * * * *

SELF-CONCEIT—Its Danger

Quintilian said of some in his time that they might have become excellent scholars had they not been so persuaded of their scholarship already. Grant, most gracious God, that I may never hold so high an opinion of my own spiritual health as to prevent my being in very deed full of Thy grace and fear!

* * * * * *

SELF-DISSATISFACTION—A Spur

"During the nine years that I was his wife," says the widow of the great artist Opie, "I never saw him satisfied with one of his productions, and often, very often, have I seen him enter my sitting-room, and throwing himself in an agony of despondence on the sofa, exclaim, 'I never, never shall be a painter as long as I live!'" It was a noble despair, such as is never felt by the self-complacent daubers of signboards, and it bore the panting aspirant up to one of the highest niches in the artistic annals of his country. The selfsame dissatisfaction with present attainments is a potent force to bear the Christian onward to the most eminent degree of spirituality and holiness.

* * * * * *

SEASON—A Convenient

The countryman when he wanted to cross the river and found it was deep, sat down by the bank to wait till the water had gone past. He waited, but the river was just as deep after all his waiting. And with all your delay, the difficulties in the way of your accepting Christ do not become any the less. If you look at the matter rightly, you will see there are no great difficulties in the way, nor were there ever such obstacles as your imagination pictures.

Another countryman having to cross Cheapside, one morning, was so confused by the traffic of omnibuses and cabs, and people, that he felt sure he could not get across then, so he waited until the people and traffic thinned, but all day long it was the same. Unless he had waited till the evening, he would have found little difference. Oh friends, you have waited for a convenient season to become a Christian, and after all your delay, the way is no clearer.

* * * * * *

SELF-ESTEEM

Self-esteem is a moth which frets the garments of virtue. Those flies, those pretty flies of self-praise, must be killed, for if they get into your pot of ointment they will spoil it all. Forget the past; thank God who has made you pray so well; thank God who has made you kind, gentle or humble; thank God who has made you give liberally; but forget it all and go forward, since there is yet very much land to be possessed.

* * * * * *

SCEPTICISM

A profession of scepticism is often nothing more than the whistling of the boy as he goes through the church-yard and is afraid of ghosts, and therefore "whistles hard to keep his courage up." They try to get rid of the thought of God because of that ghost of conscience which makes cowards of them all.

* * * * * *

SHAME—Bravely Borne

I heard of a prayer the other day which I did not quite like at first, but there is something in it after all. The good man said, "Lord, if our hearts are hard, make them soft; but if our hearts are too soft, make them hard." I know what he meant, and I think I can pray that last prayer for some of my friends who are so delicate that a sneer would kill them. May the Lord harden them till they can despise the shame!

Answer shame by making it see that you are ashamed of the scorner. Laugh at the laughter of fools, despise their despising. With glorious greatness of spirit Jesus remained unprovoked amid the cruel taunts of godless men. Run through the ribald throng. Shut your ears and run, despising the shame.

* * * * * *

SERMONS—BAD, NOT TO BE LISTENED TO

Who thrusts his arm into the fire because its flame is brilliant? Who knowingly drinks from a poisoned cup because the beaded bubbles on the brim reflect the colors of the rainbow? As we would not be fascinated by the azure hues of a serpent, so neither should we be thrown off our guard by the talents of an unsound theologian. To hear or read sufficiently to judge, is allowable to the man who, by reason of use, has had his senses exercised to discern, and whose business it is to warn others; but where error is manifest upon the surface, to expose our minds to its pernicious influence is as great a madness as to test the strength of the fever by lying in its lair. Godly, scriptural teaching is surely not so rare that we need go down to Egypt for help; there are streams enough in Israel without our drinking of the polluted water of Sihor.

* * * * * *

SECOND COMING

You grow uneasy because nearly two thousand years have passed since His ascension, and Jesus has not yet come;

but you do not know what had to be arranged for, and how far the lapse of time was absolutely necessary for the Lord's design. Those are no little matters which have filled up the great pause; the intervening centuries have teemed with wonders.

* * * * * *

SECOND COMING

It is quite clear that men will not be universally converted when Christ comes, because if they were so they would not wail. (Rev. 1:7)

* * * * * *

SECOND COMING

If I begin to describe our hope, I must begin with what, I think, is always the topmost stone of it—the hope of the second advent of our Lord and Savior Jesus Christ; for we believe that when He shall appear we shall also appear with Him in glory.

To use an ecclesiastical term, we stand between two Epiphanies; the first is the manifestation of the Son of God in human flesh in dishonor and weakness; the second is the manifestation of the same Son of God in all His power and glory.

* * * * * *

SECOND COMING

As workmen are moved to be more diligent in service when they hear their master's footfall, so, doubtless, saints are quickened in their devotion when they are conscious that He whom they worship is drawing near. He has gone away to the Father for a while, and so He has left us alone in this world; but He has said, "I will come again and receive you unto Myself," and we are confident that He will keep His word.

* * * * * *

SECOND COMING

Whenever the coming of our Lord shall be—and oh that it were today, for we never wanted Him more than now!—whenever His second advent shall take place, it shall not be a dishonor to the Church, but it will be her glory to triumph with the King at her head.

* * * * * *

SERVING GOD—The Sure Reward of

When Calvin was banished from ungrateful Geneva, he said, "Most assuredly if I had merely served man, this would have been a poor recompense; but it is my happiness that I have served Him who never fails to reward His servants to the full extent of His promise."

* * * * * *

SILENCE

If an enemy has said anything against your character, it will not always be worth while to answer him. Silence has both dignity and argument in it. Nine times out of ten, if a boy makes a blot in his copy-book and borrows a knife to take it out, he makes the mess ten times worse; and as in your case there is no blot after all, you need not make one by attempting to remove what is not there. All the dirt that falls upon a good man will brush off when it is dry; but let him wait till it is dry, and not dirty his hands with wet mud.

* * * * * *

SIN—May be Committed by Proxy

According to an old writer, no Capuchin among the Papists may take or touch silver. This metal is as great an anathema to them as the wedge of gold to Achan, at the offer whereof they start back as Moses from the serpent; yet the monk has a boy behind him who will receive and carry home any quantity, and neither complain of metal nor measure. Such are those who are great sticklers themselves for outward observance in religion, but at the same time compel their servants to sin on their account. They who sin by substitute shall be damned in person.

* * * * * *

DESIRE FOR SIN

As the young duck which has been reared in a dry place yet takes to the water as soon as it sees a pond, so do many hasten to evil at the first opportunity. How often it happens that those young persons who have been most shut out from the world have become the readiest victims of temptation when the time has come for them to quit the parental roof.

* * * * * *

BINDING SIN

Experience has taught the wise observer that sin may be bound by sin, and one ruling passion may hold the rest in check. One man is kept from licentiousness by covetousness; he would be glad to revel in vice if it were not so expensive; another would be a rake and a spendthrift, but then it would not be respectable, and thus his pride checks his passions. This restraint of sin by sin is no proof that the nature is one jot the better, but that it puts on a fairer appearance, and is more likely to deceive.

* * * * * *

SIN—How to Overcome

Sin is to be overcome, not so much by maintaining a direct opposition to it, as by cultivating opposite principles.

Would you kill the weeds in your garden, plant it with good seed: if the ground be well occupied there will be less need of the labor of the hoe.　If a man wished to quench fire, he might fight it with his hands till he was burnt to death; the only way is to apply an opposite element.—*Andrew Fuller.*

* * * * * *

SIN—Punishment of

What a diabolical invention was the "Virgin's kiss," once used by the fathers of the Inquisition! The victim was pushed forward to kiss the image, when, lo, its arms enclosed him in a deadly embrace, piercing his body with a hundred hidden knives.　The tempting pleasures of sin offer to the unwary just such a virgin's kiss.　The sinful joys of the flesh lead, even in this world, to results most terrible, while in the world to come the daggers of remorse and despair will cut and wound beyond all remedy.

* * * * * *

SIN—The Toil of It

Henry Ward Beecher says, "There was a man in the town where I was born who used to steal all his firewood. He would get up on cold nights and go out and take it from his neighbor's woodpiles. A computation was made, and it was ascertained that he spent more time and worked harder to get his fuel, than he would have been obliged to if he had earned it in an honest way, and at ordinary wages. And this thief is a type of thousands of men who work a great deal harder to please the devil than they would have to work to please God."

* * * * * *

SIN—Loved

A mouse was caught in a trap, the other day, by its tail, and the poor creature went on eating the cheese.　Many men are doing the same; they know that they are guilty and they dread their punishment, but they go on nibbling at their beloved sins.

* * * * * *

SINNERS—New Creatures

I expect that if you go into the business of mending yourself you will be like the man who had an old gun and took it to the gunsmith, and the gunsmith said, "Well, this would make a very good gun if it had a new stock and a new lock and a new barrel." So you would make a very good man by mending if you had a new heart and a new life, and were made new all over, so that there was not a bit of the old stuff left. It will be easier, a great deal, depend upon it, even for God to make you new than to mend you. What is wanted is that you should be made a new creature in Christ Jesus.

* * * * * *

SINNERS—Madness of

A recent traveller, relating the incidents of his voyage to India, writes:—"Flocks of greedy albatrosses, petrels, and Cape pigeons, crowded around the ship's stern. A hook was baited with fat, when upwards of a dozen albatrosses instantly rushed at it, and as one after another was being hauled on deck, the remainder, regardless of the struggles of the captured, and the vociferations of the crew, kept swimming about the stern. Not even did those birds which were indifferently hooked and made their escape, desist from seizing the bait a second time." Thus to the letter do ungodly men rush at the baits of Satan; they see others perish, but remain careless, and even when they are all but destroyed themselves they persist in their infatuation.

* * * * * *

SCEPTICS

Time was, whenever I heard a sceptical remark, I felt wounded and somewhat shaken. I am no longer shaken by these wandering winds. There are certain things I am as sure of as of my own existence; I have seen, tasted and handled them, and I am past being argued out of them by those who know nothing about them.

* * * * * *

SLANDER—To Be Despised

One of our ancient nobility had inscribed over his castle gate these words, which we commend to all persons who are thin-skinned in the matter of private gossip or public opinion:

They say.
What do they say?
Let them say.

* * * * * *

SLANDER—How to Overcome It

Some person reported to the amiable poet Tasso that a malicious enemy spoke ill of him to all the world. "Let him persevere," said Tasso, "his rancor gives me no pain. How much better is it that he should speak ill of me to all the world, than that all the world should speak ill of me to him."

* * * * * *

SOUL-WINNING

When a sportsman goes out after game, he does not know which way he will go, neither does he bind himself in that matter. If he is deer stalking he may have to go up the mountain side, or down the glen, across the burn, or away among the heather.

Where his sport leads him, he follows; and so it is with the genuine soul-winner: he leaves himself free to follow his one object. He does not know where he is going, but he does know what he is going after. He lays himself out for the winning of souls for Jesus. On the railway he speaks to anyone who happens to be put in the same carriage; or in the shop he looks out for opportunities to impress a customer. He sows beside all waters, and in all soils. He carries his gun at half-cock, ready to take aim at once. That is the man whom God is likely to bless.

* * * * * *

SORROW—For Sin, Absorbing

When that famous statesman Mirabeau died, all France bewailed his loss, and men for some hours could think or speak of little else. A waiter in one of the restaurants of the Palais Royal, after the manner of his race, saluted a customer with the usual remark, "Fine weather, Monsieur." "Yes, my friend," replied the other, "very fine; but Mirabeau is dead."

If one absorbing thought can thus take precedence of every other in the affairs of life, is it so very wonderful that men aroused to care for the life to come should be altogether swallowed up with grief at the dread discovery that they are by reason of sin condemned of God?

* * * * * *

SPECULATIONS—Their Folly

While a minister of my acquaintance was riding in a railway carriage, he was saluted by a member of an exceedingly litigious and speculative sect. "Pray, sir," said the sectary, "what is your opinion of the seven trumpets?" "I am not sure," said the preacher, "that I understand your question, but I hope you will comprehend mine: what think you of the fact that your seven children are growing up without God and without hope? You have a Bible-reading in your house for your neighbors, but no family prayer for your children." The nail was fastened in a sure place, enough candor of mind remained in the professor to enable him to profit by the timely rebuke.

It were greatly to be desired that Christians who are so much given to speculate upon the prophecies, would turn their thoughts and leisure to the perishing myriads by whom we are surrounded, and sow in the fields of evangelization rather than in the cloudland of guess-work interpretation.

* * * * * *

SPIRIT OF GOD—THE FIRE FROM HEAVEN

Suppose we saw an army sitting down before a granite fort, and they told us that they intended to batter it down, we might ask them, "How?" They point to a cannon ball. Well, but there is no power in that; it is heavy, but not more than half-a-hundred of perhaps a hundredweight; if all the men in the army hurled it against the fort they would make no impression. They say, "No, but look at the cannon!" Well, but there is no power in that. A child may ride upon it; a bird may perch in its mouth. It is a machine, and nothing more. "But look at the powder." Well, there is no power in that; a child may spill it; a sparrow may peck it. Yet this powerless powder and powerless ball are put in the powerless cannon; one spark of fire enters it, and then, in the twinkling of an eye, that powder is a flash of lightning, and that cannon ball is a thunderbolt which smites as if it had been sent from heaven.

So is it with our church or school machinery of this day; we have the instruments necessary for pulling down strongholds, but O for the fire from heaven!

* * * * * *

STARVING SOULS

The experiment of the Frenchman who had just brought his horse to live on a straw a day when it died, is being repeated among us, faith being literally starved to death. What low diet do some men prescribe for their souls. Marrow and fatness they do not even smell at!

* * * * * *

STRENGTH—In Touching God

We are to be like that fabled giant whom Hercules could not overcome for a long while, because he was a child of the earth, and every time he was thrown down he touched his mother earth, and rose with fresh strength. Hercules had to hold him aloft in his arms and then strangle him. Now, whenever you are thrown down and touch God in your faintness and weakness, you will find that He restoreth your soul. "To them that have no might He increaseth their strength."

* * * * * *

SUBMISSION—To the Divine Will

Payson was asked, when under great bodily affliction, if he could see any particular reason for this dispensation. "No," replied he, "but I am as well satisfied as if I could see ten thousand, God's will is the very perfection of all reason."

* * * * * *

SUFFERING—True Service

Old Betty was converted late in life, and though very poor, was very active. She visited the sick; out of her own poverty she gave to those who were still poorer; collected a little money from others when she could give none of her own, and told many a one of the love of the Savior. At last she caught cold and rheumatism, and lay in bed month after month, pain-worn and helpless.

A good minister went to see her, and asked, if after her active habits she did not find the change very hard to bea "No, sir, not at all. When I was well, I used to hear the Lord say day by day, 'Betty, go here; Betty, go there; Betty, do this; Betty, do that'; and I used to do it as well as I could; and now I hear him say every day, 'Betty, lie still and cough.' "—*James Hamilton, D.D.*

* * * * * *

TEMPTATION

Now you are content to be a Christian; satisfied to mix with poor people in holy service; quite pleased at an opportunity of teaching in a ragged school. Ah! but there may come a moment when Satan will show you the kingdoms of this world, and he will say, "All these will I give thee if thou wilt fall down and worship me"; and you may feel as if the service of Christ was not, after all, very respectable; that you could do better in the world; find choicer company, enter more select society. But drive, drive these carrion-crows away.

* * * * * *

TEMPTATIONS—Everywhere

Men who live in London need not go across the street to meet the devil. The very atmosphere of a great city is close and hot with the reek of sin. As flies in summer, so will temptations torment you, go where you may. Men of business, you need not ask for temptations; they are thick in every trade; they multiply like gnats. They swarm in the factory, the countinghouse, the exchange, and the shop.

The Christian man in public need not sigh for temptations; they will not be ashamed to solicit him in the open streets. This age tests the backbone of every Christian. A man need be a man at such an hour as this. We must not be dwarfs nor spiritual consumptives now. We have come into the very thick of the fight, and woe to that man who cannot endure temptation; but blessed is the man who can bear it even to the end.

* * * * * *

TIME—Marches on

The pendulum swings to and fro, advancing and retreating, but yet there is a real progress made; you cannot see it by watching the pendulum, but up higher on the face of the clock there is evidence of an onward march and of a coming hour. The kingdom of God is coming; righteousness shall prevail.

* * * * * *

TEMPTATIONS

One of the ancient fathers, we are told, had, before his conversion, lived with an ill woman, and some little time after, she accosted him as usual. Knowing how likely he was to fall into sin, he ran away with all his might, and she ran after him, crying, "Wherefore runnest thou away? It is I." He answered, "I run away because I am not I. I am a new man."

* * * * * *

THE LORD—A Sight of

That holy man, Mr. Walsh, when the Lord revealed Himself to him, was obliged to cry, "Hold, Lord! remember I am but an earthen vessel; and if I have more of this delight I must die." One said he would like to die of that disease, and I am very much of his mind. They say, "See Naples and die"; but to improve on it, another said, "See Naples and live"; and truly this is the better sight of the two. I would fain see my Lord so as to live to His praise. Oh, for such a vision as should shape my life, my thought, my whole being, till I become like my Lord!

TROUBLES

A Scotch saint said that when they met in the moss, or by the hillside, and were harried by Claverhouse and his dragoons, Christ was present at the sacraments in the heather much more than He ever was afterwards when they got into the kirk, and sat down quietly.

Our worst days are often our best days, and in the dark we see stars that we never saw in the light. So we will not care a pin what it is that may befall us here, so long as God is with us, and our faith in Him is genuine. Christian people, I am not going to condole with you, but I congratulate you on your troubles, for the cross of Christ is precious.

* * * * * *

TROUBLE—Needed

Speaking of a Norwegian summer, the Rev. H. Macmillan says:—"The long daylight is very favorable to the growth of vegetation, plants growing in the night as well as in the day in the short but ardent summer. But the stimulus of perpetual solar light is peculiarly trying to the nervous system of those who are not accustomed to it. It prevents proper repose and banishes sleep.

"I never felt before how needful darkness is for the welfare of our bodies and minds. I longed for night, but the farther north we went, the farther we were fleeing from it, until at last, when we reached the most northern point of our tour, the sun set for one hour and a half. Consequently, the heat of the day never cooled down, and accumulated until it became almost unendurable at last. Truly for a most wise and beneficent purpose did God make light and create darkness. 'Light is sweet, and it is a pleasant thing to the eyes to behold the sun.' But darkness is also sweet, it is the nurse of nature's kind restorer, balmy sleep, and without the tender drawing round us of its curtains the weary eyelid will not close, and the jaded nerves will not be soothed to refreshing rest.

"Not till the everlasting day break, and the shadows flee away, and the Lord Himself shall be our light, and our God our glory, can we do without the cloud in the sunshine, the shade of sorrow in the bright light of joy, and the curtain of night for the deepening of the sleep which God gives His beloved."—*Rev. Hugh Macmillan's* "Holidays on High Lands."

* * * * * *

TROUBLES—OUR GLORY

There is no glory in being a feather-bed soldier, a man bedecked with gorgeous regimentals, but never beautified by a scar, or ennobled by a wound. All that you ever hear of such a soldier is that his spurs jingle on the pavement as he walks. There is no history for this carpet knight. He is just a dandy. He never smelt gunpowder in his life; or if he did, he fetched out a smelling bottle, to kill the offensive odor. Well, that will not make much show in the story of nations. If we could have our choice, and we were as wise as the Lord Himself, we should choose the troubles He has appointed us, and we should not spare ourselves a single pang.

* * * * * *

TRUTH—FIDELITY TO THE

As the Roman sentinel in Pompeii stood to his post even when the city was destroyed, so do I stand to the truth of the atonement though the Church is being buried beneath the boiling mud-showers of modern heresy.

Everything else can wait, but this one truth must be proclaimed with a voice of thunder. Others may preach as they will, but as for this pulpit, it shall always resound with the substitution of Christ. "God forbid that I should glory, save in the cross of our Lord Jesus Christ." Some may continually preach Christ as an example, and others may perpetually discourse upon His coming to glory: we also preach both of these, but mainly we preach Christ *crucified*, to the Jews a stumblingblock, and to the Greeks foolishness; but to them that are saved Christ the power of God, and the wisdom of God.

* * * * * *

TRUTH—Very Personal

There went a man out of this place one evening who was spoken to by one of our friends, who happened to know him in trade, and held him in good repute. "What! have you been to hear our minister tonight?" The good man answered, "Yes, I am sorry to say I have." "But," said our friend, "why are you sorry?" "Why," he said, "he has turned me inside out, and spoiled my idea of myself. When I went into the Tabernacle I thought I was the best man in Newington, but now I feel that my righteousness is worthless."

"Oh," said the friend, "that is all right; you will come again, I am sure. The Word has come home to you, and shown you the truth: You will get comfort soon." That friend did come again, and he is here tonight: he takes pleasure in that very truth which turned him inside out; and he comes on purpose that the Word of the Lord may search him, and try him, and be to him as a refiner's fire.

* * * * * *

UNBELIEF—Wickedness of

The late Dr. Heugh, of Glasgow, a short time before he breathed his last, said, "There is nothing I feel more than the criminality of not trusting Christ without doubt—

without doubt. Oh, to think what Christ is, what He did, and whom He did it for, and then not to believe Him, not to trust Him! There is no wickedness like the wickedness of unbelief!"

* * * * * *

WARNINGS

A very skilful bowman went to the mountains in search of game. All the beasts of the forest fled at his approach. The lion alone challenged him to combat. The bowman immediately let fly an arrow, and said to the lion, "I send thee my messenger, that from him thou mayst learn what I myself shall be when I assail thee." The lion thus wounded rushed away in great fear, and on a fox exhorting him to be of good courage, and not to run away at the first attack: "You counsel me in vain, for if he sends so fearful a messenger, how shall I abide the attack of the man himself?"

If the warning admonitions of God's ministers fill the conscience with terror, what must it be to face the Lord Himself? If one bolt of judgment bring a man into a cold sweat, what will it be to stand before an angry God in the last great day?

* * * * * *

WHOLE-HEARTEDNESS

I have seen boys bathing in a river, in the morning. One of them has just dipped his toes in the water, and he cries out as he shivers, "Oh, it's so cold!" Another has gone in up to his ankles, and he also declares it is awfully chilly. But see, another takes a header from the bank, and rises all in a glow; all his blood is circulating, and he cries "Delicious! What a fine morning; I am all in a glow. The water is splendid!" That is the boy for enjoying a bath.

You, Christian people, who are paddling about in the shallow of religion, and just dipping your toes into it, you stand shivering in the cold air of the world which you are afraid to leave. Oh, that you would plunge into the river of life, how it would brace you; what tone it would give you! In for it, young man, in for it! Be a Christian out and out. Serve the Lord with your whole being. Give yourself wholly to Him who bought you with His blood. Plunge into the sacred blood of grace, and you will exclaim:

"Oh this is life: oh, this is joy,
My God, to find Thee so;
Thy face to see, Thy voice to hear,
And all Thy love to know."

* * * * * *

WOMEN—Preaching

When Boswell told Johnson one day that he had heard a woman preach that morning at a Quaker's meeting, Johnson replied, "Sir, a woman preaching is like a dog walking on his hind legs. It is not done well; but you are surprised to find it done at all." We will add that our surprise is all the greater when women of piety mount the pulpit, for they are acting in plain defiance of the Holy Spirit, written by the pen of the apostle Paul.

* * * * * *

WORD—Ways of Treating It

There are two ways of treating the seed. The botanist splits it up, and discourses on its curious characteristics; the simple husbandman eats and sows; sows and eats. Similarly there are two ways of treating the gospel. A critic dissects it, raises a mountain of debate about the structure of the whole, and relation of its parts; and when he is done with his argument, he is done; to him the letter is dead; he neither lives on it himself, nor spreads it for the good of his neighbors; he neither eats nor sows. The disciple of Jesus, hungering for righteousness, takes the seed whole; it is bread for today's hunger, and seed for tomorrow's supply.—*W. Arnot.*

* * * * * *

WORLD—Deception of

Aesop's fable says:—"A pigeon oppressed by excessive thirst, saw a goblet of water painted on a sign-board. Not supposing it to be only a picture, she flew towards it with a loud whirr, and unwittingly dashed against the sign-board, and jarred herself terribly. Having broken her wings by the blow, she fell to the ground, and was killed by one of the bystanders."

The mockeries of the world are many, and those who are deluded by them not only miss the joys they looked for, but in their eager pursuit of vanity bring ruin upon their souls. We call the dove silly to be deceived by a picture, however cleverly painted, but what epithet shall we apply to those who are duped by the transparently false allurements of the world!

* * * * * *

WORLD—Its Instability

Queen Elizabeth once said to a courtier, "They pass best over the world who trip over it quickly; for it is but a bog: if we stop, we sink."

* * * * * *

ZEAL—Causing Unity

There was a blacksmith once who had two pieces of iron which he wished to weld into one, and he took them just as they were, all cold and hard, and put them on the anvil, and began to hammer with all his might, but they were two pieces still, and would not unite. At last he remembered what he ought never to have forgotten; he thrust both of them into the fire, took them out red-hot, laid the one upon the other, and by one or two blows of the hammer they very soon became one.

* * * * * *

SPURGEON'S GOLD

The following pages contain quotations taken from the original works of C. H. Spurgeon. These were selected and published originally by Rev. Edmond Hez Swem, pastor Second Baptist Church, Washington, D. C., in the year 1888, in a book bearing the above title. We have chosen the best from over 2400 original selections made by Dr. Swem.

As the reader feasts upon these vivid and practical "sentence sermons" we believe he will agree with us that no writer of ancient or modern times (apart of course, from the inspired writers of the Holy Scriptures) can surpass in forceful, epigrammatic prose the pen of Charles Haddon Spurgeon.—D. O. F.

SHORT SAYINGS

A cake made of memories will do for a bite now and then, but it makes poor daily bread.

* * * * * *

A Faith that never wept is a faith that never lived.

* * * * * *

A Faith-look at Jesus breaks the heart both *for* sin and *from* sin.

* * * * * *

If the devil never roars, the church will never sing.

* * * * * *

If we were a little slower we should be quicker.

* * * * * *

I have heard of Latter-day Saints; I far more admire Every-day Saints.

* * * * * *

Periodical godliness is perpetual hypocrisy.

* * * * * *

Peace and rest are two names for a flower which buds on earth, but is only found full-bloom in heaven.

* * * * * *

Saintly souls should not be lodged in filthy bodies.

* * * * * *

Sin in satin is as great a rebel as sin in rags.

* * * * * *

The approbation of God is more than the admiration of nations.

The Cross is the last argument of God.

* * * * * *

The lance with which we reach the hearts of men is that same lance which pierced the Savior's heart.

* * * * * *

The Lord is never voiceless except to the earless soul.

* * * * * *

There is music without words: and there is prayer without words.

* * * * * *

Who wants to paddle about in a duck pond all his life? Launch out into the deep.

* * * * * *

Man's security is the devil's opportunity.

* * * * * *

Men may fast from bread that they may gorge themselves on pride.

* * * * * *

Look you well to your integrity, and the Lord will look to your prosperity.

* * * * * *

Christian! do not dishonor your religion by always wearing a brow of care.

* * * * * *

Brother, hush that murmur, natural though it be, and continue a diligent pupil in the College of Content.

* * * * * *

The spade of trouble digs the reservoir of comfort deeper, and makes more room for consolation.

Children of light may for a time walk in the darkness of sorrow.

* * * * * *

It is an awful thing for a man to go from hell to hell; to make this world a hell and then find another hell in the next world!

* * * * * *

In the struggle of life a cheerful fearlessness is a grand assistance.

* * * * * *

Skillful mariners sail by all winds, and we ought to make progress through all circumstances.

* * * * * *

Sinners may go unpunished for many a bright hour of the morning of life, but as the day grows older the shadows fall and their way is clouded over.

* * * * * *

Suppose an accident should take away our lives; I smile as I think that the worst thing that could happen would be the best thing that could happen. If we should die, we should but the sooner be "forever with the Lord."

* * * * * *

Your non-searching of the Scriptures, your weariness under Gospel preaching, your want of care to understand the mind of God, is prima facie evidence that there is some enmity in your heart against the Most High.

* * * * * *

There is no having influence over the great men or the little men of this age except by being firm in your principles and decided in what you do. If you yield an inch you are beaten; but if you will not yield—no, not the splitting of a hair—they will respect you.

We are soon coming out of the eggshell of time, and when we break loose into eternity and see the vastness of the divine purposes, we shall be altogether amazed at the service bestowed, which will be the reward of service done.

* * * * * *

He who boasts of being perfect is perfect in folly.

* * * * * *

Let a man get the light of God streaming into his soul, convincing him of sin, of righteousness, and of judgment to come and all reliance upon self in any form will seem to him to be the most hateful of crimes.

* * * * * *

Ah! if that question, "If ye love Me," needed to be raised in the sacred college of the twelve, much more must it be allowed to sift our churches and to test ourselves.

* * * * * *

As long as one Bible remains the empire of Satan is in danger.

* * * * * *

In the dogmas of modern thought there is not enough mental meat to bait a mouse-trap; as to food for a soul, there is none of it; an ant would starve on such small grain. No atonement, no regeneration, no eternal love, no covenant; what is there worth thinking upon?

* * * * * *

Remember that we have no more faith at any time than we have in the hour of trial.

* * * * * *

God thinks no better of a tree for being burdened with rotten fruit, nor of a Church for being swollen in numbers by base pretenders.

Though sinful thoughts rise, they must not reign.

* * * * * *

A man fresh from a revival meeting looks like a zealous Christian; but see him when he goes to market. As a face rendered red by the fire soon loses all its ruddiness, so do numbers lose all their godliness when they quit the society of the godly.

* * * * * *

The master-magnet of the Gospel is not fear, but love. Penitents are drawn to Christ rather than driven. The most frequent impulse which leads men to Jesus is hope that in Him they may find salvation. Love wins the day. One hair from the head of love will draw more than the cable of fear.

* * * * * *

Do not be all sugar, or the world will suck you down; but do not be all vinegar, or the world will spit you out.

* * * * * *

Lord, save me from sins which call themselves little.

* * * * * *

When your dog loves you because it is dinner-time, you are not sure of him; but when somebody else tempts him with a bone and he will not leave you, though just now you struck him, then you feel that he is truly attached to you. We may learn from dogs that true affection is not dependent upon what it is just now receiving.

* * * * * *

We know many persons who are always doing a great deal and yet do nothing—fussy people, people to the front in every movement, persons who could set the whole world right, but are not right themselves. Very eminent men are these!

Christ did not come to scare us from sin, but to save us from it.

* * * * * *

He is a fool, writ large, who knows not God.

* * * * * *

Labor to impress thyself with a deep sense of the value of the place to which thou art going. If thou rememberest that thou art going to heaven, thou wilt not sleep on the road. If thou thinkest that hell is behind thee and the devil pursuing thee thou wilt not loiter.

* * * * * *

The ugliest sight in the world is one of those thoroughbred loafers.

* * * * * *

I have found by long experience that nothing touches the heart like the cross of Christ.

* * * * * *

There will be no climbing the hill of the Lord without effort; no going to glory without the violence of faith. I believe that the ascent to heaven is still as Bunyan described it—a staircase, every step of which will have to be fought for.

* * * * * *

Idle men tempt the devil to tempt them.

* * * * * *

When the time cometh for the Lord to make bare His arm, we shall see greater things than these, and then we shall wrap our faces in a veil of blushing confusion to think that we ever doubted the Most High.

* * * * * *

He is making his own damnation sure if he is robbing his creditors and yet professing to be a Christian.

Somewhere or other in the worst flood of trouble there always is a dry spot for contentment to get its foot on, and if there were not it would learn to swim.

* * * * * *

No flies will go down your throat if you keep your mouth shut, and no evil speaking will come up.

* * * * * *

Am I an earnest laborer together with God, or am I, after all, only a laborious trifler, an industrious doer of nothing, working hard to accomplish no purpose of the sort for which I ought to work, since I ought to live unto my Lord alone?

* * * * * *

Many people are born crying, live complaining, and die disappointed.

* * * * * *

A scare is not a conversion. A sinner may be frightened into hypocrisy, but he must be wooed to repentance and faith.

* * * * * *

It is a wretched business for a man to call himself a Christian, and have a soul which never peeps out from between his own ribs. It is horrible to be living to be saved, living to get to Heaven, living to enjoy religion, and yet never to live to bless others and ease the misery of a moaning world.

* * * * * *

O Lord, save me from all deceit and, above all, prevent my deceiving myself.

* * * * * *

O Lord, Thy Logos is my logic; Thy Testament is my argument; Thy Word is my warrant.

It is not ours to improve the Gospel, but to repeat it when we preach, and obey it when we hear.

* * * * * *

Grin and bear it is the old-fashioned advice, but sing and bear it is a great deal better.

* * * * * *

There is such a thing as carrying the cross till you are so accustomed to it that you would be almost uneasy without it.

* * * * * *

A lie to our fellow-men is meanness, but a lie to God is madness.

* * * * * *

When the pure Gospel is not preached God's people are robbed of the strength which they need in their life-journey.

* * * * * *

When a door has to be shut to save life, there is no use in half shutting it. If a person may be killed by going through it, you had better board it up, or brick it up. I want to brick up the dangerous opening of self-confidence, for it leads to deception, disappointment, and despair.

* * * * * *

He who found a Moses to face Pharaoh, an Elijah to face Jezebel, can find a man to confront the adversaries of today.

* * * * * *

But some will say that they cannot help having bad thoughts; that may be, but the question is, Do they hate them or not?

* * * * * *

There is something nobler in falling by the woodman's strokes than in perishing by a little worm at the root. The meanness of decaying into corruption while standing in the midst of a Church is awful.

* * * * * *

He who is a moral monster was not always such. By sinning much he learned to sin more.

* * * * * *

From henceforth let no man trouble me with doubts and questionings; I bear in my soul the proofs of the Spirit's truth and power, and I will have none of your artful reasonings.

* * * * * *

What is the daffodil without its golden crown, or the crocus without its cup of sunshine? Such is man without the object of his life.

* * * * * *

The introduction of a holy thought into carnal minds is a miracle as great as to get a beam of light into a blind eye or a breath of life into a dead body.

* * * * * *

When a man is proud as a peacock—all strut and show—he needs converting himself before he sets up to preach to others.

* * * * * *

Selfishness is never worse than when it puts on the garb of religion.

* * * * * *

Sinners take more pains to go to hell than the saints to go to heaven.

* * * * * *

I never yet saw a minister worth his salt who had not some crotchet or oddity.

Oh, be not Judas to Him who is Jesus to you!

* * * * * *

This is the spirit out of which fiends are made; first, neglect, then omission, then treachery and rebellion.

* * * * * *

God is in love with you. I think Aristotle said that it was impossible for one to be assured of another's love without feeling some love in return. I am not sure about that; but I think it is quite impossible to enjoy a sense of God's love without returning it in a measure.

* * * * * *

One thing I have made up my mind to; whether I find present joy or present sorrow, present commendation or present censure, I will be faithful to my Lord.

* * * * * *

Temptation to sin is no sin, for in Him was no sin, and yet He was tempted. If you yield to the temptation, therein is sin; but the mere fact that you are tempted, however horrible the temptation, is no sin of yours.

* * * * * *

I have been weakly cheered by a large number of brethren who have greatly sympathized with me and helped me to fight the Lord's battles by bravely looking on!

* * * * * *

The man that abhors evil and injustice; the man that would do good if it cost him his earthly all; the man who would not do wrong though the world should be his reward for doing it—this is the man who walks in the light, and he is the man that shall have fellowship with God and a sense of cleansing from sin.

You that are tempted of the devil; you that are troubled by mysterious whisperings in your ear; you that, when you sing or pray, have a blasphemy suggested to you; you that even in your dreams start with horror at the thoughts that cross your minds, be comforted, for your Lord knows all about temptation!

* * * * * *

In days to come you will bless God for the clouds and the darkness, since through them your tried faith grew into strong faith and your strong faith ripened into full assurance. Doubtless faith will make our nights the fruitful mothers of brighter days.

* * * * * *

It is a happy day when a full Christ and empty sinners meet.

* * * * * *

Wherever there is a self-satisfaction which is afraid of light we suspect that the rat of hypocrisy is not far off.

* * * * * *

When the world pretends to love, understand that it now hates you more cordially than ever and is carefully baiting its trap to catch you and ruin you.

* * * * * *

The wicked shall find that there are special sorrows for them—whips of scorpions for them, especially when they get farther on in life, and their youthful fires burn down to a black ash. Woe unto sinners when they have to reap the fruits of their evil deeds!

* * * * * *

It is a pleasant sight to see anybody thanking God; for the air is heavy with the hum of murmuring, and the roads are dusty with complaints and lamentations.

Some men would wish to have themselves written down at a very high figure, but a cipher is quite sufficient.

* * * * * *

We have those around us who seem to think that great grace can only display itself by raving and raging. The religion of the quiet Jesus was never intended to drive us to the verge of insanity.

* * * * * *

Surely there is more righteousness in trusting the Lord than in all the works of the flesh.

* * * * * *

No joy can excel that of the soldier of Christ; Jesus reveals Himself so graciously and gives such sweet refreshment that the warrior feels more calm and peace in his daily strife than others in their hours of rest.

* * * * * *

Sin may be exhausted, the race may be numbered, time may be finished, and need may be ended, but mercy endureth forever.

* * * * * *

He who does not long to know more of Christ knows nothing of Him yet. Whoever hath sipped this wine will thirst for more, for although Christ doth satisfy, yet it is such a satisfaction that the appetite is not cloyed but whetted.

* * * * * *

No dish ever comes to a table which is so nauseous as cold religion. Put it away. Neither God nor man can endure it.

* * * * * *

Willful people make up their mind, and then pray; and this is sheer hypocrisy.

Whenever a man is about to stab religion he usually professes very great reverence for it. Let me beware of the sleek-faced hypocrisy which is armor-bearer to heresy and infidelity.

* * * * * *

God gives none up until they fatally resolve to give themselves up, and even then His good Spirit strives within them as long as it is possible to do so, consistently with His holiness.

* * * * * *

Hang up self-confidence on a gallows high as that whereon Haman was suspended, for it is an abominable thing.

* * * * * *

Oh, the depravity of our nature! Some doubt whether it is total depravity. It deserves a worse adjective than that.

* * * * * *

Man's pride may carry him far if he is a great fool; but let him not suffer his pride to carry him into hell, for it certainly will never carry him out again.

* * * * * *

Long ago my experience taught me not to dispute with anybody about tastes and whims.

* * * * * *

This great city (London) is like a seething caldron, boiling and bubbling up with infamous iniquity.

* * * * * *

My will has fallen into God's will as a brook falls into a river.

* * * * * *

You and your sins must part, or God and you cannot be friends.

Language is a poor vehicle of expression when the soul is on fire; words are good enough things for our cool judgment, but when thoughts are full of praise they break the back of words.

* * * * * *

There is no shield for a guilty soul like the blood-red shield of the atonement.

* * * * * *

You may lose a great deal for Christ, but you will never lose anything by Christ. You may lose for time, but you will gain for eternity; the loss is transient, but the gain is everlasting.

* * * * * *

Nobody is so wise but he has folly enough to stock a stall at Vanity Fair.

* * * * * *

We must be willing to hook on anywhere; be leader or shaft-horse; be first or last; be sower or reaper, as the Lord ordains. Have no choice, and then you will find satisfaction.

* * * * * *

It is more necessary for us that we should make a discovery of our faults than of our virtues.

* * * * * *

The very things which men most dread, namely, the falling of mountains and the gaping open of the earth, will become the desire of terrified sinners at the last.

* * * * * *

It will be an awful thing to be mere empty barrels, and never know it till death deals a blow with his rod of iron and we answer to it with hollow sounds of despair.

I have sometimes wished that I had nothing else to do but to dwell with God in prayer, praise and preaching. Alas! one has to come down from the mount of the transfiguration and meet the lunatic child and the quarrelsome scribes at the bottom of the hill.

* * * * * *

An aged woman once said that if the Lord Jesus Christ really did save her, He should never hear the last of it. Join with her in that resolve.

* * * * * *

In one single moment, aye, while the clock is ticking, Jesus Christ can take the scales from a blind man's eyes and let in such a flood of daylight that he shall see heaven itself.

* * * * * *

I confess it very quietly, but I have often wished that I had a little congregation, that I might watch over every soul in it; but now I am doomed to an everlasting dissatisfaction with my work, for what am I among so many?

* * * * * *

If you know these two things—yourself a sinner and Christ a Savior—you are scholar enough to go to heaven.

* * * * * *

Surely, the devils themselves would at the first have scarce believed it, that there could exist a race of creatures so hardened as to refuse the love which visits them in grace.

* * * * * *

If you do not mean to serve Christ, at least stand out of the road and let other people serve Him.

There's no use in lying down and doing nothing because we cannot do everything as we should like.

* * * * * *

Correcting for the press is work which has to be done with great care, since thousands of copies will be faulty if the proof-sheet be not as it should be. So should the minister of a congregation be seriously earnest to be right, because his people will imitate him. Like priest, like people; the sheep will follow the shepherd.

* * * * * *

If one Christian man is right in never joining a Christian church, then all other Christian men would be right in not doing so, and there would be no visible Christian church.

* * * * * *

All men are sinners; to most men, however, sin appears to be a fashion of the times, a necessity of nature, a folly of youth, or an infirmity of age, which a slight apology will suffice to remove.

* * * * * *

God save us all from wives who are angels in the streets, saints in the church, and devils at home.

* * * * * *

Nobody speaks so sternly against sin as Jesus and those who believe His gospel; but yet it forever stands true, "This man receiveth sinners."

* * * * * *

The world is no fool; it would not be so fierce against us if it did not see something about us contrary to itself; its enmity, therefore, is part evidence that we are the children of God.

The Gospel, the whole Gospel, and nothing but the Gospel, must be our religion or we are lost men.

* * * * * *

Eggs are eggs, but some are rotten; and so hopes are hopes, but many of them are delusions. Hopes are like women, there is a touch of angel about them all—but there are two sorts.

* * * * * *

Snails leave their slime behind them, and so do vain thoughts.

* * * * * *

This Bible is our treasure. We prize each leaf of it. Let us bind it in the best fashion, in the best morocco of a clear intelligent faith; then let us put a golden clasp upon it, and gild its edges by a life of love, and truth, and purity, and zeal. Thus shall we commend the volume to those who have never looked within its pages.

* * * * * *

Either give up sin or give up hope.

* * * * * *

A frightened sinner is a sinner still.

* * * * * *

Trust in self is a disloyal attempt upon the crown rights of the Redeemer. All those doings and willings and feelings are a setting up of self-salvation.

* * * * * *

I have on several occasions felt everything like fear of dying taken from me simply by the process of weariness; for I could not wish to live any longer in such pain as I then endured.

Perseverance in prayer is necessary to prevalence in prayer.

* * * * * *

Despite our ignorance, nothing can go wrong while the Lord in infinite knowledge ruleth over all. The child playing on the deck does not understand the tremendous engine whose beat is the throbbing heart of the stately Atlantic liner, and yet all is safe; for the engineer, the captain and the pilot are in their places and well know what is being done. Let not the child trouble itself about things too great for it.

* * * * * *

A man had better be shut up with a bear robbed of her whelps than live with an accusing conscience. No racks or fires can equal the misery of being consciously guilty and seeing no way of escape from sin.

* * * * * *

The further a man goes in lust and iniquity the more dead he becomes to purity and holiness; he loses the power to appreciate the beauties of virtue or to be disgusted with the abominations of vice.

* * * * * *

I hardly know of a more conscious union between a man and Christ than that which is effected when in sinking times the grip of the crucified hand is felt as our sole rescue from death.

* * * * * *

I have noticed old people whose memories have been sadly feeble. I knew one who forgot his children. But I never knew an old saint yet who forgot the name of the Savior or failed to remember His love.

The sermon that only gets as far as the ear is like a dinner eaten in a dream.

* * * * * *

Surely it ill becomes us to waste a penny, an hour, or an opportunity. Let us be severely economical for the Lord our God.

* * * * * *

Anger does a man more hurt than that which made him angry. It opens his mouth and shuts his eyes and fires his heart and drowns his sense and makes his wisdom folly.

* * * * * *

Those who preach not the atonement exhibit a dumb and dummy gospel; a mouth it hath and speaketh not; they that make it are like unto their idol.

* * * * * *

Some are hindered in their usefulness by their great dignity.

* * * * * *

I am always afraid of the tail end of a habit. A man who is always in debt will never be cured till he has paid the last sixpence.

* * * * * *

Two little words are good for every Christian to learn and to practice—pray and stay. Waiting on the Lord implies both praying and staying.

* * * * * *

If there is but a step between you and death—if the Judge is at the door—go and wind up your little difficulties. You that have family quarrels, wipe them out. You that have any malice in your heart, turn it out.

* * * * * *

Prating does not make saints, or there would be plenty of them.

A man that lives without prayer ought not to live.

*   *   *   *   *   *

The terrible acts of the Lord are few, but no age is quite left without them, for the Lord liveth still, and He is evermore the same.

*   *   *   *   *   *

It is as easy to make an idol out of your own thoughts as it is for the Hindoo to make a god of the mud of the Ganges.

*   *   *   *   *   *

The Lord's providence rules words as well as deeds, and makes men say the right words without their knowing why they say them.

*   *   *   *   *   *

Those who preach the cross of our Lord Jesus are the terror of modern thinkers. In their heart of hearts they dread the preaching of the old fashioned Gospel, and they hate what they dread.

*   *   *   *   *   *

When a man is no longer afraid, but is prepared to welcome whatever comes, because he sees in it the appointment of a loving Father, why, then he is in a happy state.

*   *   *   *   *   *

I am unable to frame an excuse for profane language; it is needless, willful wickedness. Men talk so as to horrify us; they chill our blood with fear lest God should take them at their word, and all for nothing at all.

*   *   *   *   *   *

Calm resignation does not come all at once; often long years of physical pain, or mental depression, or disappointment in business, or multiplied bereavements are needed to bring the soul into full submission to the will of the Lord.

We incline to attach undue importance to matters which are proper and useful in their places, but which are by no means essential to salvation.

* * * * *

Those who seek after the novelties of this conceited century seek to push their Lord from His place that a philosopher may fill His throne.

* * * * * *

If you ever allow yourself to be pleased by those who speak well of you, to that extent will you be capable of being grieved by those who speak ill of you.

* * * * * *

The powers of darkness are not so strong as they seem to be. The subtlest infidels and heretics are only men. What is more, they are bad men; and bad men at bottom are weak men.

* * * * * *

Whenever you find sickness in a house or death in a darkened chamber, seize the opportunity to speak for your Lord. Your voice for truth will be likely to be heard, for God Himself is speaking and men must hear Him whether they will or no.

* * * * * *

The more God blesses you, the less you shall see of any adequate reason in yourself why you should be blest.

* * * * * *

The moment the Lord Jesus Christ saves a soul He gives that soul strength for its appointed service.

* * * * * *

Always have something in hand that is greater than your present capacity. Grow up to it, and when you have grown up to it, grow more.

To you is given not gold, nor silver, nor precious stones to fashion, but immortal spirits that shall glorify Christ on earth and in heaven.

* * * * * *

The Gospel is not sent to men to gratify their curiosity by letting them see how other people get to heaven. Christ did not come to amuse us, but to redeem us.

* * * * * *

The devil can use humility for his purpose as well as pride. Whether he makes us think too much or too little of our work, it is all the same to him, so long as he can get us off from it.

* * * * * *

I am sometimes startled at the power of a feeble prayer to win a speedy answer.

* * * * * *

The life of a genuine Christian is a perpetual miracle, which could be wrought by none but the Lord God.

* * * * * *

When ungodly men are tempted the bait is to their taste, and they swallow it greedily. Temptation is a pleasure to them; indeed, they sometimes tempt the devil to tempt them.

* * * * * *

Sooner than let their tongues have a holiday men would complain that the grass is not a nice shade of green, and say that the sky would have looked neater if it had been whitewashed.

* * * * * *

Find, if you can, one occasion in which Jesus inculcated doubt, or bade men dwell in uncertainty.

Death can hide in a drop and ride in a breath of air. Our greatest dangers lie hidden in little things.

* * * * * *

We care little for those who are orthodox Christians in creed if it is clear that they are heterodox in life. He who believes the truth should himself be true.

* * * * * *

One pampered sin will slay the soul as surely as one dose of poison will kill the body.

* * * * * *

Everyone can see that there is a grave distinction between sins of infirmity and willful transgressions. A man may splash us very badly with the wheel of his carriage as he passes by, and we may feel vexed, but the feeling would have been very much more keen if he had thrown mud into our face with deliberate intent.

* * * * * *

The keeping of every word of God is indispensable.

* * * * * *

Here is a man that was lately a drunkard, and God has loved him and made him sober, and he is wonderfully proud because he is sober. What folly! Have done, sir! have done! Give God the glory of your deliverance from the degrading vice, or else you are still degraded by ingratitude.

* * * * * *

By and by you and I will have to die, unless the Lord should suddenly come.

* * * * * *

From a sweet fountain of thought we shall have sweet waters of talk.

We never know what strength is till our own weakness drives us to trust omnipotence; never understand how safe our refuge is till all other refuges fail us.

* * * * * *

He who is not godly every day is not godly any day.

* * * * * *

Sermons which we have studied with care, delivered with travail, prayed over and wept over, are praised for such minor matters as taste, accuracy and diction, and the truth they contain is not received.

* * * * * *

The best doctors are Dr. Diet, Dr. Quiet and Dr. Merryman.

* * * * * *

Since the Lord has appeared to me, He has made me see His restraining hand where once I saw nothing but the cruel disappointment of my hopes.

* * * * * *

Before you begin a thing make sure it is the right thing to do; ask Mr. Conscience about it. Do not try to do what is impossible; ask Common Sense.

* * * * * *

Deep sincerity breeds in a man a blessed indifference to the judgments of men.

* * * * * *

Adversity is the richest field in all the farm of life.

* * * * * *

Love the soul of every man with all the intensity of thy being.

Many people would like to go to heaven by an underground railway; secrecy suits them.

* * * * * *

God has been very merciful to some of us in never letting money come rolling in upon us, for most men are carried off their legs if they meet with a great wave of fortune. Many of us would have been bigger sinners if we had been trusted with larger purses.

* * * * * *

Religion must not be like a fine piece of medieval armor, to be hung upon the wall, or only worn on state occasions. No; it is a garment for the house, the shop, the bank.

* * * * * *

To say there is a God is not much. It is the same as to say there is a bank; but there may be a bank, and you may be miserably poor. There certainly is a God, but that God may be no source of comfort to you. The joy of the whole thing lies in that word "my." *My* God will hear me.

* * * * * *

He who talks forever about himself has a foolish subject, and is likely to worry and weary all around him.

* * * * * *

Stick to your calling, plod on, and be content; for, make sure, if you can *undergo* you shall *overcome*.

* * * * * *

The most abominable beings out of hell are Christians without Christianity; and there are plenty of them.

* * * * * *

The Lord Jesus always owns a faith which comes toward him, however lame it may be.

To draw Him nearer to me, and myself nearer to Him, is the innermost longing of my soul.

* * * * * *

Let all the necessities of men impel you, compel you, constrain you to be blessing them.

* * * * * *

The world is always looking to the Church, not so much to hear her teachings as to see her doings.

* * * * * *

Happy is the man who is happy in his wife. Let him love her as he loves himself, and a little better, for she is his better half.

* * * * * *

I would not have a converted person wait a week before trying to do something for Jesus. Run as soon as you find your feet.

* * * * * *

He will certainly come in His own person to reward His saints; and ere He comes He sees what you are doing. If this does not nerve you to tireless diligence in holy service, what can?

* * * * * *

When old age comes on and memory fails me, that which my soul shall hold as a death grip will not be historical remembrance, classical lore, or theological learning, but what she knows by inward experience of the Lord her God.

* * * * * *

London is worse than a wilderness to many; a man may lay himself down and die in these streets and nobody will care for him. The millions will pass him by, not for want of kindness, but from want of thought. There is no such horrible wilderness as a wilderness of men.

A fool soon makes up his mind, because there is so very little of it; but a wise man waits and considers.

* * * * * *

The right thing is to feel that the more God loves you the more you love Him; the more He does for you the more will you do for Him.

* * * * * *

It is better to be a good housewife, or nurse, or domestic servant, than to be a powerless preacher or a graceless talker.

* * * * * *

London is a simmering caldron of vice and crime.

* * * * * *

There is one person who plagues you; if you could only get away from him, you would be content; but that person happens to be yourself, and there appears to be no rest for you, either in company or in solitude.

* * * * * *

Even the thoughtless or trifling repetition of the Name of the Lord involves great sin, for thus a man taketh the sacred Name in vain, yet men trifle with that Name in common conversation, and that with fearful frequency.

* * * * * *

Studying the lives of eminent men, we come to this conclusion; that on the whole it is good for a man to bear the yoke; good for a man to breast the billows; good for a man to pass through fire and through water, and so to learn sublime lessons.

* * * * * *

When you feel most unfit to resort to God you may still go to Him, for He is your fitness and your physician.

God's children always play the fool when they play the judge; they are never in order when they act as if they were the head of the family of grace.

* * * * * *

No signs can be more alarming than the growing infidelity and worldliness which I see among those who call themselves Christians.

* * * * * *

I might curse myself seven times deep by a prayer within the next seven minutes, if there were no safeguards and limits to the promise of prayer being answered.

* * * * * *

Consciences used to work up and down, yes or no; but now they have an eccentric action, altogether indescribable. A man serves the devil nowadays and gets the devil's pay, and all the while talks of serving God.

* * * * * *

In grace you can be under bonds, yet not in bondage. I am in the bonds of wedlock, but I feel no bondage; on the contrary, it is a joy to be so bound. The bond of grace is a marriage bond, uniting us to Him whom we love above all, even the altogether lovely Bridegroom of our souls.

* * * * * *

Do what the Lord bids you, when He bids you, where He bids you, as He bids you, as long as He bids you, and do it at once.

* * * * * *

Nothing hardens like the Gospel when it is long trifled with. To lie asoak in the truth without receiving it into the heart is sure destruction.

I would sooner be a cat on hot bricks or a toad under a harrow than let my own children be my masters.

* * * * * *

A man of God is not prepared to enjoy success till he has tasted defeat.

* * * * * *

Religious deceivers are the worst of vermin.

* * * * * *

Remember that your own thoughts of what God is are far from being correct unless they are drawn from His own revelation.

* * * * * *

Might not the Lord stand in a prayer-meeting and hear a dozen of us talk our piece and never say, "Behold, he prayeth?"

* * * * * *

Happy is the man who has been enabled to endure; he rises from the deeps of woe like a pearl-finder from the sea, rich beyond comparison.

* * * * * *

There are no loose threads in the providence of God, no stitches are dropped, no events are left to chance. The great clock of the universe keeps good time, and the whole machinery of Providence moves with unerring punctuality.

* * * * * *

There are fools enough in the world, and there can be no need that Christian men should swell the number.

* * * * * *

If you cannot get on honestly, be satisfied not to get on.

* * * * * *

Love thyself less and less and love thy God more.

Your frothy professors quote Dickens or George Eliot, but God's afflicted quote David or Job.

* * * * * *

You can sin yourself into an utter deadness of conscience, and that is the first wage of your service of sin.

* * * * * *

While you are brother to the worm and akin to corruption, you are, nevertheless, nearly related to Him who sitteth on the eternal throne.

* * * * * *

Sometimes our corrupt nature quarrels with God about our service. The Lord says, "Go into the Sunday school." "I should have liked to preach," says the young man. "Go into the Sunday school." "Not so, Lord," says he, and he will not go, and thus he misses his life-work. It will not do for us to choose what work we will do.

* * * * * *

Those who boast of perfection will have much to grieve over when once they come to their senses and stand in truth before the living God.

* * * * * *

If we are to be acceptable before God there must be no keeping up of favorite sins—no sparing of darling lusts—no providing for secret iniquities; our service will be filthiness before God if our hearts go after our sins.

* * * * * *.

It is ill to be a saint without and a devil within.

* * * * * *

They say a brain is worth little if you have not a tongue; but what is a tongue worth without a brain?

Demons that gather about our last hour shall flee away as bats fly out of a cavern scared by a torch; they shall flee when they hear the voice, "Behold, he prayeth."

* * * * * *

If a fellow takes the trouble to flatter he expects to be paid for it, and he calculates that he will get his wages out of the soft brains of those he tickles.

* * * * * *

If you hunt the butterfly of wealth too eagerly you may spoil it by the stroke with which you secure it.

* * * * * *

He has gained more than he has lost, even though he has lost everything, if he has gained contentment, conformity to the will of God, a deep experience, and a surer hope.

* * * * * *

Draw not the beloved bodies to the cemetery with dreary pomp and with black horses, but cover the coffin with sweet flowers and drape the horses with emblems of hope. It is the better birthday of the saint, yea, his truer wedding-day. Is it sad to have done with sadness? Is it sorrowful to part with sorrow?

* * * * * *

He promised to come to die, and He kept His word; He now promises to come to reign, and be you sure that He will keep His tryst with His people.

* * * * * *

If you come to Christ I do not care how you come, for I am sure you could not have come at all if the Father had not drawn you; and if He has drawn you, there is no mistake in your method of coming.

How often have I seen the invalid, who might almost long for death, draw out a long existence of continuous pain, while the man who shook your hand with a powerful grip and stood erect like a column of iron is laid low of a sudden and is done.

* * * * * *

I have no doubt that much sorrow might be prevented if words of encouragement were more frequently spoken fitly and in season; and therefore to withhold them is sin.

* * * * * *

I believe there are thousands of men who could go to the stake and die, or lay their necks on the block to perish with a stroke for Christ, who nevertheless find it hard work to live a holy, consecrated life.

* * * * * *

Where do they bury the bad people? Right and left in our churchyard; they seem all to have been the best of folks, a regular nest of saints; and some of them so precious good it is no wonder they died—they were too fine to live in such a wicked world as this.

* * * * * *

We have never reaped such a harvest from any seed as from that which fell from our hand while tears were falling from our eyes.

* * * * * *

The pent-up misery and the seething sin of London may yet produce a second edition of the French Revolution unless the grace of God shall interpose.

* * * * * *

When a man's religion all lies in his saving his own self and in enjoying holy things for his own self there is a disease upon him.

We count the thought of the present moment to be methodical madness, Bedlam out of doors; and those who are furthest gone in it are credulous beyond imagination.

* * * * * *

There is no dynasty to follow His dynasty; no successor to take up the crown of our Melchisedec. My immortal spirit rejoices in the hope of rendering endless homage to the eternal King.

* * * * * *

That atheistic philosophy which makes the whole world to be a chance production which grew of itself, or developed itself by some innate force, is a very dreary piece of friction to the man who delights himself in the Almighty.

* * * * * *

The worst sort of clever men are those who know better than the Bible, and are so learned that they believe that the world had no Maker, and that men are only monkeys with their tails rubbed off.

* * * * * *

This century's philosophy will one day be spoken of as an evidence that softening of the brain was very usual among its scientific men.

* * * * * *

The devil does not mind having half your heart. He is quite satisfied with that, because he is like the woman to whom the child did not belong; he does not mind if it be cut in halves.

* * * * * *

The indifference to Scripture is the great curse of the Church at this hour.

Wherein I sin, that is my own; but wherein I act rightly, that is of God, wholly and completely.

* * * * * *

No ignorance is so terrible as ignorance of the Savior.

* * * * * *

Good men suffer when they are tempted, and the better they are the more they suffer.

* * * * * *

If I had to die like a dog I should still wish to live the life of a Christian.

* * * * * *

Do not attempt to go sneaking to heaven along some back lane; come into the King's highway; take up your cross and follow Him. I would persuade you to an open confession.

* * * * * *

To live without Christ is not life, but a breathing death.

* * * * * *

The man who begins to exult over his fallen brother is the likeliest man to fall himself.

* * * * * *

Do not treat God's promises as if they were curiosities for a museum, but use them as every-day sources of comfort.

* * * * * *

Lord, whether I live long or not, I leave to Thee; but help me to live while I live that I may live much. Thou canst give life more abundantly; let me receive it, and let my life be filled, yea, packed and crammed, with all manner of holy thoughts and words and deeds to Thy glory.

It is an empty heart that the devil enters. You know how the boys always break the windows of empty houses; and the devil throws stones wherever the heart is empty.

* * * * * *

If thou hast a faith which looks to ceremonies, creeds, prayers, and feelings it will fail thee when most thou needest help.

* * * * * *

We must preach the coming of the Lord, and preach it somewhat more than we have done, because it is the driving power of the Gospel.

* * * * * *

Some fools are left alive to write on the monuments of those who are buried.

* * * * * *

We have never reached the sum of our grace-given privileges till we are more at home with God than with any one else in the universe.

* * * * * *

Too much cunning overdoes its work, and in the long run there is no craft which is so wise as simple honesty.

* * * * * *

Sanctified trouble has a great tendency to breed sympathy, and sympathy is to the church as oil to machinery.

* * * * * *

Inside a man's heart there is need of a thorough plowing by God's grace, for if any part of our nature is left to itself the weeds of sin smother the soul.

* * * * * *

A world where everything was easy would be a nursery for babies, but not at all a fit place for men.

History must repeat itself so long as we have the same human nature to deal with, the same sins to ensnare mankind, the same truth to be trifled with, and the same devil to stir men up to the same mischief.

* * * * * *

What a discovery it will be when, having struggled through one life of sorrow, you shall find yourself beginning another life of greater sorrow, which will never come to an end.

* * * * * *

There will come to godly men, sometimes, temptations to sin. The purest have been tempted to impurity; the most devout have been tempted to blaspheme; men full of integrity have been tempted to dishonesty, and the most truthful to falsehood.

* * * * * *

Certain men never get on in business; they do not like their trade, and so they never prosper. And certainly, in the matter of religion, no man can ever prosper if he does not love it, if his whole heart is not in it.

* * * * * *

Of all the devils in the world I hate a roaring devil least; but a fawning devil is the worst devil that ever a man meets.

* * * * * *

It were a blessed thing to go through fifty hells to heaven if such a thing could be.

* * * * * *

Weakness hurries, rages, shouts, for it has need to do so. Strength moves with its own deliberate serenity and effects its purpose.

Do not kick against suffering, for in so doing you may be fighting against God.

* * * * * *

What have we to do with consequences? It is ours to do the right, and leave results with the Lord.

* * * * * *

O child of God, death hath lost its sting, because the devil's power over it is destroyed! Then cease to fear dying.

* * * * * *

One word of God is like a piece of gold, and the Christian is the gold-beater, and can hammer that promise out for whole weeks.

* * * * * *

Christ exempts you from sin, but not from sorrow. Remember that, and expect to suffer.

* * * * * *

Christian, meditate much on heaven; it will help thee to press on, and to forget the toil of the way.

* * * * * *

It is the easiest thing in the world to give a lenient verdict when one's self is to be tried; but O, be just and true here. Be just to all, but be rigorous to yourself.

* * * * * *

What whips of burning wire will be yours when conscience shall smite you with all its terrors!

* * * * * *

Cautious pilots have no desire to try how near the quicksand they can sail, or how often they may touch a rock without springing a leak; their aim is to keep as nearly as possible in the midst of a safe channel.

If we indulge in any confidence which is not grounded on the Rock of Ages our confidence is worse than a dream.

* * * * * *

How unwisely do those believers talk who make preferences in the Persons of the Trinity.

* * * * * *

We should all know more, live nearer to God, and grow in grace, if we were more alone. Meditation chews the cud and extracts the real nutriment from the mental food gathered elsewhere.

* * * * * *

We know that our enemies are attempting impossibilities. They seek to destroy the eternal life which cannot die while Jesus lives, to overthrow the citadel against which the gates of hell shall not prevail.

* * * * * *

As love comes from heaven, so it must feed on heavenly bread. It cannot exist in the wilderness unless it be fed by manna from on high. Love must feed on love. The very soul and life of our love to God is His love to us.

* * * * * *

If every day I journeyed towards the goal of my desires I should soon reach it, but backsliding leaves me still far off from the prize of my high calling and robs me of the advances which I had so laboriously made.

* * * * * *

"I am a Roman!" was of old a reason for integrity; far more, then, let it be your argument for holiness, "I am Christ's."

Go to the river of thine experience and pull up a few bulrushes and plait them into an ark, wherein thine infant faith may float safely on the stream. Forget not what thy God has done for thee.

* * * * * *

This alone is the true life of a Christian—its source, its sustenance, its fashion, its end, all gathered up in one word—CHRIST JESUS.

* * * * * *

He who follows Christ for his bag is a Judas; they who follow for loaves and fishes are children of the devil; but they who attend Him out of love to Himself are His own beloved ones.

* * * * * *

You are meddling with Christ's business and neglecting your own when you fret about your lot and circumstances.

* * * * * *

The first promise ran thus: "The seed of the woman," not the offspring of the man. Since venturous woman led the way in the sin which brought forth Paradise lost, she, and she alone, ushers in the Regainer of Paradise.

* * * * * *

Though dishonest as the thief, though unchaste as the woman who was a sinner, though fierce as Saul of Tarsus, though cruel as Manasseh, though rebellious as the prodigal, the great heart of love will look upon the man who feels himself to have no soundness in him, and will pronounce him clean when he trusts in Jesus crucified.

* * * * * *

More wealth brings more care, but more grace brings more joy.

A man may have too much money or too much honor, but he cannot have too much grace.

* * * * * *

Tale-bearing emits a threefold poison; for it injures the teller, the hearer and the person concerning whom the tale is told.

* * * * * *

God's smile and a dungeon are enough for a true heart; His frown and a palace would be hell to a gracious spirit.

* * * * * *

Sin may drag thee ever so low, but Christ's great atonement is still under all. You may have descended into the deeps, but you cannot have fallen so low as "the uttermost"; and to the uttermost He saves.

* * * * * *

Let us move in the common affairs of life with studied holiness, diligence, kindness and integrity.

* * * * * *

To forget to praise God is to refuse to benefit ourselves; for praise, like prayer, is one great means of promoting the growth of the spiritual life. It helps to remove our burdens, to excite our hope, to increase our faith.

* * * * * *

Sincere repentance is continual. Believers repent until their dying day.

* * * * * *

Some Christians are living *on* Christ, but are not so anxious to live *for* Christ.

* * * * * *

A true prayer is an inventory of wants, a catalogue of necessities, a revelation of hidden poverty.

The best of men are conscious, above all others, that they are men at the best.

* * * * * *

We shall never find happiness by looking at our prayers, our doings, or our feelings; it is what *Jesus* is, not what we are, that gives rest to the soul.

* * * * * *

Ungodly persons and mere professors never look upon religion as a joyful thing; to them it is service, duty, or necessity, but never pleasure or delight.

* * * * * *

Let us not imagine that the soul sleeps in insensibility. "Today shalt thou be with Me in Paradise," is the whisper of Christ to every dying saint.

* * * * * *

Be content to live unknown for a little while, and to walk your weary way through the fields of poverty or up the hills of affliction, for by and by you shall reign with Christ.

* * * * * *

Every individual believer is precious in the sight of the Lord; a shepherd would not lose one sheep, nor a jeweler one diamond, nor a mother one child, nor a man one limb of his body, nor will the Lord lose one of His redeemed people.

* * * * * *

Above all other seasons a man needs his God when his heart is melted within him because of heaviness.

* * * * * *

Men turn their faces to hell and hope to get to heaven; why don't they walk into the horse-pond and hope to be dry?

Lord, let me never be what I cannot be forever.

* * * * * *

Princes should behave as princes. Their haunts should be in palaces and not amid dung-heaps. How, then, is it that some who profess and call themselves Christians are found raking in questionable amusements to discover pleasure, and many others groping amid sordid avarice to find satisfaction in wealth?